FAITH VANGUARD

THE URGENT CALL TO AWAKEN AMERICA

SCOTT FARLEY

TABLE OF CONTENTS

Dedication — vii
Introduction — ix

Chapter 1 — 1
The Battle Lines Are Drawn

Chapter 2 — 15
The World Without God

Chapter 3 — 31
The Vanishing of Truth

Chapter 4 — 44
The Quiet Collapse

Chapter 5 — 54
The Cost of Clarity

Chapter 6 — 64
When Faith Becomes Quiet

Chapter 7 — 72
The Cost of Standing

Chapter 8 — 81
The Battle for the Next Generation

Chapter 9 — 90
When Truth Is Labeled Hate

Chapter 10 — 98
Rebuilding What Was Lost

Chapter 11 — 108
The Rise of a Remnant

Chapter 12 — 121
The Cost of Conviction

Chapter 13 — 138
Building a Faith Vanguard

Chapter 14 — 154
Becoming the Leaders the Future Needs

Chapter 15 — 170
The Future We Are Called to Build

Chapter 16 — 184
The Line That Separates the Watchers from the Builders

Epilogue — 201

About the Author	207
Faith Vanguard — The Next Step	209
A Letter to the Reader	213
A Closing Blessing	215

Published by Faith Vanguard Publishing

Copyright © 2026 Scott Farley

All rights reserved.

No part of this book may be reproduced, distributed, or transmitted in any form or by any means—electronic or mechanical—without prior written permission from the publisher, except for brief quotations used in reviews or scholarly works.

Scripture references are paraphrased unless otherwise noted.

This book is not affiliated with, endorsed by, or sponsored by any political party, organization, or institution. It represents the author's convictions regarding faith, obedience, and responsibility in the face of modern spiritual battles.

This book is for informational and inspirational purposes only. It does not constitute legal, medical, or professional advice. The author and publisher assume no responsibility for actions taken based on the content of this book.

ISBN: 979-8-9941936-0-0 (Paperback)

ISBN: 979-8-9941936-2-4 (eBook)

ISBN: 979-8-9941936-1-7 (Hardcover)

First Edition

Printed in the United States of America

DEDICATION

To the faithful remnant—

Those who stand firm in the trenches,
refusing to surrender ground to darkness.

The warriors who daily put on the full armor of God,
choosing obedience over comfort,
truth over approval,
and courage over compromise—

even when it costs everything.

This is for you

INTRODUCTION
THE STAND WE MUST TAKE

America is not collapsing because it rejected God. It is collapsing because it learned how to live as if God does not matter.

This is far more dangerous than atheism.

Atheism argues. Apathy erodes.

A nation can survive an enemy. It cannot survive forgetting what it exists for.

In 2026, churches still gather. Worship songs still rise. Politicians still quote Scripture when it benefits them. But something far more destructive has taken root beneath the surface: faith has been stripped of its authority and reduced to a private hobby.

We still talk about Jesus. We no longer live as if He is King.

That is the real crisis.

The United States was never perfect, but it was once built on a shared assumption: there is a moral order higher than human will. Right and wrong were not created by culture; they were discovered. Freedom was not the ability to do whatever you want; it was the ability to live within truth without tyranny.

That foundation is gone.

Not by force. By forgetting.

Secularism did not need to burn Bibles. It only had to convince people that they were irrelevant. Faith could remain in buildings, in personal prayers, in sentimental traditions — just not in law, education, medicine, sexuality, or truth itself.

So, we complied.

We told ourselves we were being loving. We called it tolerance. We mistook surrender for peace.

Now we live in a nation where children are told they were born in the wrong body, criminals are rebranded as victims, and biology is treated as bigotry. A culture where truth is no longer discovered but enforced by power.

And a church that mostly stayed quiet while it happened.

This book exists because that silence has become sin.

We are not watching a political shift. We are watching a civilizational fracture — a collision between a worldview rooted in God and a worldview determined to erase Him.

Neutrality is gone.

Every parent. Every pastor. Every teacher. Every believer is already standing on one side of the line or the other.

This is not a call to anger. It is a call to clarity.

This is not about power. It is about truth.

This is not about nostalgia for the past. It is about whether there will be a future where Christ is still proclaimed without apology.

Faith Vanguard is not a brand. It is not a political movement. It is the name for those who refuse to go quietly into cultural exile.

The vanguard goes first. The vanguard takes the fire. The vanguard holds the line when others retreat.

You are either part of the sleeping church or part of the remnant.

And history is watching which one you choose.

1

THE BATTLE LINES ARE DRAWN

The most dangerous lie in modern Christianity is this: "We can just focus on loving people and stay out of all this conflict."

That lie has already cost us a generation.

Every war in history was lost by the side that did not believe it was happening. The enemy does not need to overpower a sleeping army. He only needs to keep it asleep. That is exactly what has happened to much of the Western church.

For decades, cultural change crept forward quietly — redefining marriage, erasing sexual boundaries, dissolving the authority of Scripture, and replacing God with the self. Churches adapted rather than resisted. Pastors softened rather than warned. Christians learned to be polite rather than faithful.

Now the ground beneath us has shifted so far that we barely recognize the landscape.

Schools teach children that truth is subjective. Corporations punish biblical conviction. Governments rewrite reality. Media mocks righteousness. And churches argue about tone.

This is not normal disagreement.

. . .

This is spiritual war

The apostle Paul warned us: we do not wrestle against flesh and blood, but against rulers, authorities, and powers of this present darkness. These powers do not wear uniforms. They speak through ideologies, laws, entertainment, and social pressure.

Their goal is not merely to oppose Christianity. It is to render it irrelevant.

A church that believes but does not speak. A church that gathers but does not contend. A church that sings but does not stand. That kind of church is harmless to the enemy.

So the pressure increased.

From Tolerance to Coercion

What began as "tolerance" became "affirmation." What began as "respect" became "celebration." What began as "coexistence" became "submit."

We were told: If you do not affirm, you are hateful. If you do not comply, you are dangerous. If you do not agree, you must be silenced.

That is not pluralism. That is coercion.

And it is now everywhere.

Christians are fired for refusing to use pronouns. Parents lose custody for refusing to affirm gender transitions. Pastors face investigation for preaching Scripture. Churches are pressured to rewrite doctrine or lose protection.

These are not isolated incidents. They are the battle lines.

And they are no longer moving slowly.

They are advancing.

The Seduction of Neutrality

Neutrality is the most seductive lie of every collapsing civilization. It whispers that you can keep your beliefs without living by them, that you can love Christ without ever having to choose Him when the cost is high, and that silence is wisdom while accommodation is maturity. History exposes that lie every time. No culture drifts into tyranny overnight. It slides there through compromise, through people who know something is wrong but convince themselves it is not their responsibility to speak, and through institutions that decide survival is more important than truth.

How the Church Lost Its Voice

The Western church did not lose influence because it was persecuted. It lost influence because it was comfortable. For decades, Christians were allowed to believe anything as long as those beliefs stayed out of public life. You could worship in your building, pray in private, and raise your hands on Sunday, just so long as you did not bring biblical conviction into education, law, sexuality, or culture. So a trade was made. The church received peace while the world took its children. The church received comfort while the world took its schools. The church received acceptance while the world took its voice.

What began as tolerance slowly became marginalization, and what became marginalization has now become coercion. This is always how totalizing ideologies operate. First they ask to be included. Then they demand affirmation. Finally they require obedience. We are now living in that final stage. The cost of dissent is no longer theoretical. It is measured in lost jobs, revoked licenses, custody battles, lawsuits, reputational destruction, and in some places, legal punishment.

A teacher who refuses to affirm gender ideology risks their career. A business owner who will not celebrate what Scripture calls sin risks financial ruin. A pastor who preaches the full counsel of God risks investigation and surveillance. And a Christian who stays silent risks something even greater than any of these—the slow death of their faith. Faith that is never exercised begins to atrophy. Conviction that never costs anything is eventually replaced by convenience. Belief that never faces pressure eventually fades into sentiment.

The enemy understands this dynamic perfectly. He does not need to make people hate Christ. He only needs to make them afraid to stand for Him. Fear is the true weapon of this age. Fear of being labeled. Fear of being fired. Fear of being isolated. Fear of being misunderstood. So believers begin to self-censor. They edit their words. They soften their convictions. They hide behind vague spiritual language instead of clear biblical truth. The result is a church that still exists but no longer threatens anything. And a church that threatens nothing will be ignored by the world and forgotten by history.

This is why neutrality is no longer possible. You are either resisting the cultural tide or being carried by it. You are either shaping the world around you or being reshaped by it. There is no safe middle ground between truth and lies, between Christ's authority and the culture's demands. The battle lines are not merely ideological. They are spiritual. Christ claims lordship over every part of life. The culture claims the same. One of them will have it.

The uncomfortable truth is that the Church did not wake up one morning and decide to abandon its cultural influence. It slowly surrendered it, one compromise at a time. In the decades after World War II, Christianity still held a place of moral authority in Western society. Scripture shaped law. Churches shaped communities. Families were formed around shared assumptions about marriage, sexuality, and truth. But prosperity brought something far more dangerous than persecution: distraction. Comfort weakened conviction. Entertainment replaced formation. Therapy replaced repentance. And slowly, the Church began to speak less about sin and more about self-esteem, less about holiness and more about happiness.

This shift was not always intentional. Many pastors believed they were being compassionate. Many churches believed they were becoming relevant. They thought that if they softened the message, more people would listen. What they did not realize was that when the gospel loses its sharp edges, it also loses its power. A Christ who never confronts is no Christ at all. A cross that demands nothing transforms no one. As sermons became shorter and easier, and as doctrine was replaced with motivational language, a generation grew up inside church buildings without ever being confronted by the holy God of Scripture.

At the same time, the wider culture was being catechized by new authorities. Television, movies, universities, and later social media became the primary storytellers. They taught a different gospel: that personal fulfillment is the highest good, that identity is self-constructed, and that any moral boundary that restricts desire is oppression. While churches were trying to be liked, the culture was training minds. While pastors were trimming doctrine to avoid offense, the world was discipling the next generation with relentless consistency.

The result is now visible everywhere. Millions of young adults who grew up in church no longer see any meaningful difference between Christian faith and secular spirituality. Jesus has become a brand, not a King. Worship has become entertainment, not reverence. Scripture has become a suggestion, not an authority. When those young adults encounter a culture that offers them identity, purpose, and belonging without demanding repentance, many simply drift away. They were never taught how to stand when truth became costly.

This is how a civilization changes without riots or revolutions. It happens through a slow exchange of stories. When the church stops telling the true story of God and creation and redemption with conviction, something else fills the vacuum. Secularism does not need to argue against Christianity if Christianity no longer believes in itself strongly enough to speak. The silence becomes the message. The retreat becomes the testimony.

That retreat has now ended. The culture no longer merely ignores Christian conviction. It actively resists it. Laws are written to force compliance. Institutions are redesigned to exclude biblical truth. The church is no longer allowed to simply be private. It must either submit or be punished. The season of comfortable coexistence is over, and the Church is being asked a question it cannot avoid: will you obey God, or will you preserve your place in the world?

Every believer now lives on a front line, whether they realize it or not. Parents feel it when schools undermine what they teach at home. Employees feel it when corporate policies demand affirmation of what Scripture denies. Pastors feel it when preaching the Word risks legal or social consequences. Even ordinary conversations carry weight that they did not a generation ago. The culture is no longer content to let Christians quietly believe. It wants them to agree.

This is the moment that separates casual faith from true discipleship. When following Christ becomes inconvenient, expensive, or socially costly, many will quietly fade. They will convince themselves that a softened Christianity is wiser, more loving, more strategic. But history is clear: a Church that trades truth for acceptance always ends up losing both.

The Moment of Personal Cost

There is a moment in every believer's life when the cost of following Christ becomes unmistakably clear. It is no longer theoretical. It is no longer something that happens to missionaries in distant countries or pastors in hostile regimes. It becomes personal. A job is threatened. A relationship is strained. A reputation is damaged. A door quietly closes. In that moment, faith stops being an idea and becomes a decision.

For much of modern Western history, Christians were spared that moment. Following Jesus carried social benefits. Church attendance brought respectability. Biblical values aligned with public norms. You could be faithful and comfortable at the same time. That era is gone. What remains is something far more honest. We are being forced to decide whether Christ is truly Lord or merely a personal preference.

Jesus warned us this would happen. He never promised cultural safety. He promised division, persecution, and cost. He said that anyone who follows Him must be willing to lose even their own life. Those words were easy to spiritualize when no one was asking for anything. They become painfully concrete when obedience threatens everything you've built.

The Church now stands in that moment collectively. We are being asked, by law and by culture, to declare what we truly believe about truth, about identity, about sin, and about God. The question is not whether we can find clever ways to avoid conflict. The question is whether we will remain faithful when avoidance is no longer possible.

This pressure is exposing something uncomfortable: many believers have never learned how to suffer. They were taught how to attend, how to volunteer, how to give, and how to sing, but not how to stand when the world turns hostile. A Christianity that has never been tested by fire often collapses when heat finally arrives. Faith that was built on convenience cannot survive conflict.

Yet this moment is not a tragedy. It is a refining. Throughout history, whenever the Church lost social power, it gained spiritual clarity. Whenever believers were forced to choose between Christ and comfort, the gospel burned brighter. Persecution has always been the anvil on which authentic faith is forged.

We are now being given that anvil again. Cultural Christianity is crumbling. Nominal faith is being shaken. What remains will be a smaller, stronger, more faithful people who know exactly what they believe and why. This is not decline. This is preparation.

The vanguard is not made up of those who are loudest or most visible. It is made up of those who will not move when pressure comes. They are parents who refuse to surrender their children to ideological systems. They are employees who refuse to lie for promotion. They are pastors who refuse to trade Scripture for safety. They are ordinary believers who quietly, steadily obey God even when it costs them.

This is what the battle lines really look like. They are not drawn on maps. They run through hearts, homes, workplaces, and churches. Every day, every believer is choosing which side of those lines they will live on.

And those choices, multiplied across millions of lives, will decide the future of the Church in this age.

One of the greatest deceptions of our time is the belief that cultural pressure can be managed through cleverness. Many Christians assume that if they just choose the right words, the right tone, or the right strategy, they can avoid the conflict that is coming. They imagine that careful compromise will preserve peace, that subtlety will protect their influence, and that quiet retreat will keep them safe.

But there is no clever way to stand against a system that demands total conformity.

Every ideological regime throughout history has followed the same pattern. It begins by tolerating dissent, then by marginalizing it, and finally by punishing it. At first, believers are simply asked to be polite. Then they are told to be affirming. Eventually, they are required to participate in what their conscience rejects. By the time resistance becomes illegal, it is already socially dangerous.

We are moving through that progression now.

Christians who would never have imagined themselves in conflict with the state are suddenly facing mandates that violate their deepest convictions. Parents who only wanted to raise their children in peace are being told they must affirm beliefs that contradict biology and Scripture. Churches that only wanted to preach the gospel are being warned that certain truths are no longer welcome in the public square.

This is not about being political. It is about being faithful.

The gospel has always disrupted the systems of the world because it declares that no authority is higher than Christ. That is why every empire, every ideology, and every totalizing worldview eventually comes into conflict with Christianity. The moment a culture demands ultimate loyalty, the Christian must refuse.

That refusal is what the world calls extremism.

But Scripture calls it obedience.

There is a quiet courage required in this moment that is far more difficult than loud activism. It is the courage to live truthfully in a world that punishes truth. It is the courage to speak plainly when euphemism would be safer. It is the courage to lose what cannot last in order to keep what cannot be taken.

This is what the vanguard embodies. They are not reckless. They are resolved. They do not seek conflict, but they do not flee from it. They understand that faithfulness is not measured by comfort but by constancy. They know that the Kingdom of God has always advanced not through cultural approval but through people who were willing to endure cultural rejection.

The battle lines are now visible to anyone willing to look. What remains is to decide where you will stand when they cross your life.

The most painful aspect of this moment is not the hostility of the culture but the confusion within the Church. Many believers sense that something is wrong, yet they have been taught for so long to avoid confrontation that they struggle to recognize when avoidance has become disobedience. They want to be loving, but they have been told that love means never disagreeing. They want to be faithful, but they have been warned that faithfulness will make them look intolerant.

This internal conflict is not accidental. It is the result of years of theological thinning. When Scripture is no longer taught as the authoritative Word of God but as one voice among many, believers lose their confidence. They begin to treat convictions as opinions and obedience as optional. In that vacuum, cultural narratives rush in to define what is good, what is loving, and what is acceptable.

A church that is unsure of its own truth cannot withstand external pressure.

That uncertainty shows up everywhere. Pastors hesitate to preach difficult passages. Christian parents are unsure how to talk to their children about sexuality and identity. Believers second-guess themselves when biblical teaching collides with cultural narratives. What once was clear has been blurred, not because Scripture has changed, but because we have stopped teaching it with courage.

Yet clarity is returning, not through revival rallies or political victories, but through conflict. Pressure has a way of stripping away illusions. When believers are forced to choose between what God says and what the culture demands, many are rediscovering what they truly believe. They are opening their Bibles again. They are praying with urgency. They are forming communities of conviction. They are becoming, often quietly and painfully, more rooted in Christ than they have ever been.

This is how the vanguard is formed. Not through hype, but through hardship. Not through popularity, but through perseverance. The believers who remain faithful when it costs them are the ones who will carry the gospel into whatever comes next. They will be fewer, but they will be stronger. They will be less celebrated, but they will be more anchored.

The Church is being sifted. What is being shaken cannot remain. What is being refined will endure. The question is not whether this process will happen. It is whether you will allow it to make you more faithful or more fearful.

Every generation of believers faces a moment when faith must move from theory to practice. This is ours.

There is a strange and holy clarity that comes when a believer finally accepts that following Christ will not be rewarded by the world. As long as we still hope to be liked, we will be tempted to compromise. As long as we still expect applause, we will soften the truth. But when we surrender the need for approval, we become free to obey.

This is why the early church was so powerful. They had nothing to protect. They had no status to lose. They were not trying to build a brand. They were bearing witness to a resurrection. Their lives were already surrendered, so fear had nothing left to take from them. That kind of faith is unstoppable.

We are being invited into that same freedom now. The collapse of cultural Christianity is painful, but it is also purifying. When the world stops pretending to be neutral toward faith, believers are forced to decide whether Christ is worth the cost. Those who answer yes will discover a depth of joy and clarity that comfort could never provide.

The vanguard is made up of those who no longer need the world's permission to be faithful. They do not measure success by influence or applause. They measure it by obedience. They do not ask whether standing will be popular. They ask whether it will be right.

This shift changes everything. When you are no longer afraid of losing what the world gives, you become dangerous to systems that thrive on fear. You cannot be manipulated by shame. You cannot be controlled by threat. You cannot be silenced by exclusion. Your life is already hidden with Christ in God.

That is why the enemy works so hard to keep believers distracted, divided, and discouraged. A confident, surrendered Christian is more powerful than any ideology. Not because they are loud, but because they are free.

The battle lines are not only external. They run through your heart. Will you cling to the hope of being accepted by the culture, or will you accept the freedom of belonging to Christ? One path leads to anxiety and compromise. The other leads to peace and courage.

The vanguard chooses the second.

The question before us is no longer whether the world is changing. That has already been settled. The question is whether the Church will change with it or stand apart from it. History remembers those who held fast when everything around them shifted. It forgets those who tried to keep a foot in both worlds.

Every believer now faces a defining choice. You can live quietly within the boundaries the culture allows, keeping your faith safely tucked away where it cannot offend or influence anything. Or you can live openly under the lordship of Christ, knowing that obedience will cost you something, but also knowing that it will give you something far greater.

There is no third option.

The vanguard is not waiting for permission. It is not waiting for elections, court rulings, or cultural tides to turn. It is moving now, in homes, in churches, in workplaces, and in hearts. It is made up of ordinary people who have decided that Christ is worth more than comfort, truth is worth more than approval, and obedience is worth more than safety.

This is not a movement of anger. It is a movement of conviction. It is not fueled by fear of the future, but by faith in the King who already holds it. Those who join it will not be promised ease. They will be promised something far better: the peace that comes from knowing you stood when it mattered.

The battle lines have been drawn. They run through every institution, every community, and every conscience. The culture will keep moving. The pressure will keep rising. The cost will keep increasing. But so will the glory of faithful obedience.

Where Will You Stand

The question that remains is not abstract. It is deeply personal.

Where will you stand?

Because the future of the Church in this age will be shaped by the quiet, costly, courageous decisions made by people just like you. And those decisions are being made right now, one faithful act at a time.

The vanguard has already begun to move.

The only thing left is whether you will move with it.

Prayer

Father,

We confess how easily we have loved comfort more than obedience and approval more than truth. Forgive us for the times we stayed quiet when You called us to stand. Give us courage that does not depend on circumstance and faith that does not bend to fear. Teach us to live as citizens of Your Kingdom in a world that has forgotten You. Make us faithful, not famous. Make us bold, not bitter. Make us steady when the ground shakes. In Jesus' name, Amen.

Reflection

1. Where in my life have I been tempted to stay silent in order to avoid discomfort or conflict?

2. What have I been afraid of losing if I stand openly for Christ?

3. If someone were to watch my daily choices, would they see someone shaped more by culture or by Christ?

Challenge

This week, identify one place where you have been shrinking back — a conversation, a decision, a relationship, or a truth you have avoided. Take one deliberate step of obedience there. Speak when you would normally stay silent. Refuse when you would normally comply. Pray before you act, then trust God with the outcome. The vanguard is not formed by dramatic gestures, but by faithful steps taken when no one is watching.

2

THE WORLD WITHOUT GOD

The most radical transformation of the modern world did not happen through revolutions, elections, or even wars. It happened quietly, inside the human imagination. We did not wake up one day and decide to reject God. We simply began to organize our lives as though He were unnecessary. Over time, that assumption reshaped everything—from how children are educated to how laws are written, from how families are formed to how human worth is defined.

Secularism Is Not Neutral

This shift is what secularism truly is. It is not atheism, and it is not merely skepticism. It is a worldview that treats God as irrelevant to public life. You can believe in Him privately if you want, but He must not have authority over culture, morality, science, or identity. Faith is allowed only as long as it does not interfere.

When God Is Removed, Something Replaces Him

. . .

For a time, this arrangement seemed peaceful. Christians were permitted to worship, to pray, and to gather. But beneath the surface, something far more corrosive was happening. When God is removed from the center of society, there is no neutral ground left behind. Some other authority must take His place. In our age, that authority has become human desire, human will, and human power.

The consequences are now everywhere. When there is no Creator, there is no given meaning to human life. When there is no higher law, right and wrong become matters of opinion. When there is no transcendent purpose, identity becomes something to be invented rather than discovered. The self becomes both the starting point and the final judge of truth.

Fragmentation Becomes the New Normal

This is why our culture feels so unstable. Every individual is encouraged to create their own version of reality, yet everyone is also demanded to affirm everyone else's. The result is endless conflict. What one person claims as truth another experiences as threat. What one group celebrates another is told they must honor. Without a shared moral foundation, society becomes a battlefield of competing wills.

The church was not immune to this shift. As secularism advanced, many believers unconsciously adopted its assumptions. Faith became something we added to our lives rather than the framework that defined them. We learned to compartmentalize. God belonged in church, in prayer, and in personal spirituality. But education, politics, economics, sexuality, and science were treated as neutral zones governed by purely human reasoning.

That division has never existed in biblical Christianity. Scripture does not present God as a spiritual consultant who offers advice on Sundays. It presents Him as the sovereign Lord over every inch of creation. When we accept a world where God is excluded from public life, we are not being tolerant. We are being unfaithful.

This is the world the next generation has inherited. They did not vote for it. They were born into it. They have grown up in schools that teach them they are cosmic accidents, in media that tells them their desires define them, and in institutions that treat God as a relic. Many of them still feel a hunger for meaning, but they have been trained to search for it everywhere except the One who gives it.

Understanding this cultural moment is not optional. It is the battlefield on which the future of the Church will be decided.

The result of this shift has been subtle but devastating. A society can survive disagreement about God. It cannot survive indifference toward Him. When God is removed from the center of reality, everything else begins to float. Truth becomes negotiable. Meaning becomes personal. Identity becomes self-assigned. What once felt solid now feels optional.

This is why modern culture feels so unstable. It is not because people have too many opinions. It is because there is no longer an agreed-upon source of truth above those opinions. When every individual becomes their own authority, conflict becomes inevitable. Everyone is right in their own eyes, and no one is accountable to anything beyond themselves.

Secularism promised neutrality. What it delivered was fragmentation.

In a world without God, morality no longer flows from something higher than human desire. It becomes a social contract—something negotiated, revised, and discarded whenever it becomes inconvenient. Right and wrong stop being rooted in what is true and begin to shift with what is popular. Over time, this erodes not only ethical clarity, but personal integrity. People begin to live not by what they believe, but by what costs them the least.

A Faith That Must Hide Is Already Losing

. . .

Faith, under this system, becomes decorative.

It is allowed in private spaces, but not in public ones. It is permitted in houses of worship, but not in schools, courts, or cultural institutions. Belief is tolerated so long as it remains silent. The moment it speaks with conviction, it is labeled dangerous. The moment it draws moral lines, it is accused of intolerance. The world without God does not persecute faith overtly. It simply renders it irrelevant.

And relevance, in the modern world, is power.

This is why Christians increasingly feel like strangers in their own society. They did not change. The definition of reality did. What was once assumed—that God exists, that truth is knowable, that morality is objective—has been replaced by a new story: that everything is constructed, and nothing is sacred. Under that story, faith is no longer a foundation. It is a curiosity.

Yet human beings were not designed to live in a sacred vacuum.

When God is removed, something else always rushes in to take His place. Politics becomes religion. Identity becomes doctrine. Personal feelings become ultimate truth. People still crave meaning, worship, and moral certainty—they simply redirect those longings toward substitutes that cannot bear the weight of them.

This is why cultural debates feel so apocalyptic. When nothing is anchored in God, everything becomes existential. Every disagreement becomes a battle over identity. Every policy becomes a moral crusade. Every criticism becomes a personal attack. Without a higher authority to appeal to, society turns inward, consuming itself in endless conflict.

The world without God is not peaceful.

It is anxious.

It is a world desperate for validation and terrified of judgment. A world that celebrates tolerance while growing more intolerant by the day. A world that preaches freedom while punishing anyone who refuses to conform to its shifting standards. This is not liberation. It is spiritual disorientation.

And the Church was never meant to blend into that.

The tragedy is not that secularism exists. It always has. The tragedy is that many believers have quietly accepted its assumptions. They still speak the language of faith, but they have adopted the logic of a godless world. They have begun to separate their spiritual convictions from their public lives, as if truth were something that must be hidden to survive.

But a faith that must hide is already losing.

The gospel was never designed to be a private comfort. It was a public declaration that reality itself has a King. When Christians forget that, they do not become more loving—they become more afraid. And fear is never a substitute for conviction.

The world without God is not waiting to be politely persuaded. It is actively reshaping itself around a story that leaves Him out. Every law, every institution, every cultural norm is being quietly rewritten according to that story. The question is no longer whether this is happening.

The question is whether the Church will notice in time.

What makes this moment so dangerous is not hostility toward faith, but confusion about reality itself. A culture that forgets God does not simply lose religion—it loses the lens through which it understands everything. When the Creator is removed from the story, the creation no longer knows what it is for.

This is why so many people today feel unmoored. They have more choices than any generation in history, yet less clarity about who they are. They are told they can be anything, yet they feel like nothing. Identity has become a project instead of a discovery. And projects never end—they only demand more work, more performance, more self-invention.

The Crisis Is Meaning

God's absence creates a vacuum that self must fill.

But the self is too small to bear that weight.

When people are forced to be their own source of meaning, they begin to collapse under the pressure. Every failure becomes catastrophic. Every criticism becomes unbearable. Every disappointment becomes proof that life is empty. Anxiety, depression, and despair are not random epidemics—they are the natural byproducts of a world that has cut itself off from transcendence.

A society without God still hungers for purpose. It simply does not know where to find it.

So it searches in career, in romance, in pleasure, in political causes, in identity movements, in endless distraction. These things promise meaning, but they cannot deliver it. They were never meant to. And when they fail, people do not blame the substitutes—they blame themselves. They work harder. They chase more. They reinvent again. The cycle never ends.

This is not freedom.

It is exhaustion.

The Church Must Offer a Different Story

The Church is supposed to offer something radically different: a story in which life already has meaning because it comes from God. A story in which identity is received, not manufactured. A story in which suffering is not pointless, and hope is not an illusion. But when the Church begins to mirror the world, it loses the very thing that made it powerful.

If Christianity becomes just another lifestyle option, it stops being a lifeline.

This is why the modern crisis of faith is not primarily intellectual. It is spiritual. People are not rejecting God because He has been disproven. They are ignoring Him because they have been taught they do not need Him. They have been trained to live as if the material world is all that exists and the present moment is all that matters.

Yet deep down, they know better.

No amount of comfort can erase the question of eternity. No amount of success can silence the ache for significance. No amount of entertainment can fill the longing for something beyond ourselves. These are not weaknesses—they are reminders that we were made for more.

The world without God can explain how things work.

It cannot explain why anything matters.

And when "why" disappears, so does hope.

People may still smile, still laugh, still build lives—but beneath it all there is a quiet dread that something essential is missing. That dread is not something to be medicated away. It is a signal. A signal that the soul knows it has been disconnected from its source.

This is the great lie of secularism: that humans can flourish while pretending their Creator is optional.

History proves otherwise.

Civilizations do not collapse when they lose technology. They collapse when they lose meaning. They do not fall when they lack resources. They fall when they no longer know what they are living for. And a culture that removes God from the center eventually has nothing left to hold it together.

Which is why this moment matters so much.

The question is not whether the world is changing.

It is whether the Church will remember who it is in the middle of that change.

When a culture forgets God, it does not become neutral—it becomes shaped by whatever fills the empty space. Power, pleasure, identity, and ideology rush in to take the throne. What was once sacred becomes negotiable. What was once fixed becomes fluid. And what was once rooted in truth becomes governed by whoever speaks the loudest.

This is why modern society feels so fragile. It is built on shifting ground.

Without God as the reference point, even language begins to erode. Words no longer describe reality; they are used to redefine it. Truth becomes a matter of narrative. Whoever controls the story controls what is considered normal, moral, and acceptable. This is not accidental. It is the natural outcome of a world that no longer believes in something higher than itself.

And stories are powerful.

They shape what people believe about love, about identity, about purpose, about right and wrong. They teach us what to celebrate and what to shame. When God is removed from the story, those narratives drift. They may still sound compassionate, but they slowly detach from anything that can anchor them. Over time, compassion turns into permissiveness, and permissiveness turns into confusion.

The world without God does not hate morality.

It simply keeps rewriting it.

This constant revision creates exhaustion. People are told to be endlessly tolerant, endlessly flexible, endlessly open—yet the boundaries of what is acceptable keep narrowing. One wrong word, one outdated belief, one refusal to affirm the latest ideology can make someone a pariah. In the name of freedom, conformity becomes ruthless.

And no one ever feels safe.

This is the irony of a secular age: it promises liberation, yet produces anxiety. It rejects absolute truth, yet demands absolute loyalty to its own shifting standards. It claims to celebrate diversity, yet punishes anyone who does not think the right thoughts or say the right words. A world without God has no mercy, because it has no higher standard of grace.

Only power.

This is why so many cultural battles feel so intense. They are not really about policies or preferences. They are about what story will define reality. Will we live as if humans are created in the image of God, or as if they are merely products of biology and culture? Will we treat truth as something discovered, or something constructed? Will we believe that meaning is given, or that it must be invented?

These questions are not abstract.

They shape everything.

They shape how children are taught, how families are formed, how justice is pursued, how life is valued. They shape whether suffering has purpose or is merely to be escaped. They shape whether sacrifice is noble or foolish. They shape whether faith is seen as courage or as a threat.

In a world without God, even love becomes unstable.

It is reduced to emotion, desire, or convenience. When those fade, commitment fades with them. Relationships become fragile because they are no longer grounded in something deeper than feelings. The same is true of communities. When shared belief disappears, only shared interest remains—and interest is never strong enough to hold people together for long.

This is not a moral failure as much as a spiritual one.

A society that cuts itself off from God cuts itself off from the source of meaning, coherence, and hope. What remains may look modern, free, and progressive, but underneath it is hollow. It cannot sustain itself. It cannot answer the deepest questions of the human heart.

And sooner or later, the emptiness begins to show.

One of the most revealing signs of a godless culture is how it treats human life. When God is removed, people are no longer seen as sacred—they are seen as useful. Worth becomes conditional. Value becomes something that must be earned, proven, or granted by those in power. The language of dignity remains, but its foundation disappears.

This is why modern debates about life, death, and identity feel so cold. When humans are no longer understood as creations of God, they are reduced to biological processes and social constructs. A life becomes valuable only if it is wanted. A body becomes meaningful only if it aligns with personal desire. Even suffering is treated not as something to be endured with hope, but as something to be eliminated at any cost.

This shift has quietly changed how we see one another.

People are no longer neighbors—they are categories. They are no longer souls—they are demographics. They are no longer brothers and sisters—they are allies or enemies, useful or problematic, affirming or offensive. A world without God does not know how to love people who disagree, because love has been redefined as agreement.

Yet Scripture presents a radically different vision. It declares that every human being bears the image of God, regardless of their beliefs, behavior, or brokenness. That image gives them a dignity that cannot be voted away or culturally revised. It is not earned. It is bestowed.

Without that truth, compassion becomes selective.

A secular culture will fight fiercely for the rights of some while quietly discarding others. It will champion the powerful identities of the moment while ignoring the weak, the unborn, the elderly, and the inconvenient. It will speak of justice, yet redefine it whenever it becomes uncomfortable. Justice without God becomes whatever the strongest coalition decides it is.

This is why political movements begin to look like religions. They promise redemption. They offer moral certainty. They create saints and sinners. They provide meaning in a world that has lost it. But unlike true faith, they have no grace. There is no forgiveness for heresy. There is no restoration for dissent. There is only cancellation.

And cancellation is a kind of secular excommunication.

In this environment, many believers are tempted to retreat. They want to avoid conflict. They want to keep their heads down. They hope that if they remain quiet, they can survive. But the gospel was never meant to be hidden. A truth that cannot be spoken is not a truth that can be lived.

The Church's calling has never been to mirror the culture, but to offer it something better. Not power, but truth. Not control, but hope. Not endless affirmation, but redemptive love that tells the truth about sin and grace.

A world without God cannot offer that.

Only the Church can.

And that is why it is being pressured to change.

The deeper danger of a godless world is not simply that it rejects Christian belief, but that it quietly teaches people to forget that belief ever mattered. Faith is not attacked so much as it is trivialized. It is treated as a private hobby, something quaint and outdated, rather than as a claim about reality itself. When that happens, Christianity is no longer seen as something to be opposed. It is simply something to be ignored.

This is how secularism wins without ever appearing to fight.

A culture that ignores God will still borrow His language. It will speak of love, justice, equality, and human rights. But without God, those words slowly lose their meaning. They become slogans instead of truths. They are used to advance agendas rather than to reflect something eternal. Over time, people stop asking whether something is right and begin asking only whether it is acceptable.

That shift is subtle, but it is devastating.

When acceptance becomes the highest virtue, truth becomes the greatest threat. Anything that draws moral lines is seen as dangerous. Anything that says no is labeled hateful. In this environment, the Church's message becomes increasingly uncomfortable. A gospel that speaks of sin, repentance, and redemption sounds jarring to a world that wants affirmation without transformation.

So the pressure mounts.

Believers are told to update their faith, to make it more inclusive, more flexible, more aligned with modern values. They are encouraged to keep the parts of Christianity that feel uplifting and discard the parts that feel demanding. Over time, this produces a version of faith that is easier to live with—but far harder to recognize.

It is Christianity without a cross.

A faith that never confronts is not a faith that saves. A Christ who never challenges is not the Christ of Scripture. The power of the gospel has always come from its refusal to flatter human pride. It tells us that we are deeply loved and deeply broken, that we are forgiven and called to change. A world without God wants the love without the repentance, the grace without the truth.

But grace without truth is not grace.

It is sentiment.

The Church must decide whether it will be shaped by that sentiment or stand on something firmer. The message of Christ is not designed to fit neatly into every culture. It is designed to transform them. That transformation always begins with discomfort.

This is not cruelty.

It is mercy.

A world without God is a world slowly forgetting what it means to be human. The Church exists to remind it.

And that reminder will not always be welcomed.

In a culture that no longer believes in anything higher than itself, even suffering loses its meaning. Pain becomes something to be avoided at all costs rather than something that can shape the soul. Difficulty is treated as a flaw in the system rather than a part of the human story. Without God, there is no larger purpose to endure for, and so discomfort becomes intolerable.

This is why modern life is so focused on escape. We distract ourselves from silence, from reflection, from anything that might force us to confront the deeper questions. We scroll. We binge. We numb. A world without God is often loud, not because it is joyful, but because it is afraid of stillness. Stillness might remind us that something is missing.

Yet Scripture tells a very different story about suffering. It does not deny pain, but it frames it within redemption. It teaches that trials can refine, that hardship can deepen faith, that even loss can be woven into something meaningful. When God is present, suffering does not have the final word. Without Him, it does.

This difference changes how people live.

A godless culture seeks comfort above all else, even when that comfort costs integrity, community, or truth. People are encouraged to cut off anything that causes discomfort—relationships, responsibilities, even their own pasts. But a life built around avoiding pain becomes shallow. It cannot produce resilience, gratitude, or lasting joy.

The Church is meant to stand as a quiet contradiction to that story. It proclaims that meaning is not found in avoiding suffering but in walking through it with God. It proclaims that hope is not an illusion but a promise. It offers a vision of life that is deeper than pleasure and stronger than despair.

That vision is desperately needed.

A world without God will always struggle to answer the question of why we should keep going when things fall apart. It can offer therapy, distraction, and temporary relief, but it cannot offer ultimate hope. Only a Creator who stands beyond suffering can give it context and purpose.

This is why the gospel still matters so much in a secular age. Not because it makes life easy, but because it makes it meaningful. It tells us that we are not alone, not forgotten, and not defined by our worst moments. It tells us that love is real, truth is solid, and the future is not empty.

The Church does not exist to compete with the culture's comforts. It exists to speak into the culture's emptiness.

And that emptiness is growing.

The greatest irony of a godless world is that it still longs for God. Even as it tries to push Him to the margins, the human heart continues to ache for something beyond itself. We were not made for a closed system. We were made for transcendence. We were made to know that our lives are part of a story larger than our own.

That longing never disappears. It simply gets redirected.

In a secular age, people look for transcendence in movements, in relationships, in personal achievement, in experiences that promise to make them feel alive. They give themselves to causes that offer identity and purpose. They chase moments that feel meaningful. But none of it lasts. The hunger remains, because it was never meant to be satisfied by anything created.

Only the Creator can fill it.

This is why the world without God is so restless. It is always reaching, always striving, always searching for something it cannot name. It tries to manufacture meaning through technology, through progress, through self-expression, but meaning cannot be engineered. It must be received.

The Church's role in this moment is not to retreat in fear or to shout in anger. It is to quietly, steadily offer something the world cannot give: a vision of reality in which God is present, life is purposeful, and love is anchored in something eternal. That vision will not always be popular, but it will always be needed.

A culture that has forgotten God is not beyond hope.

It is simply starving.

The gospel is not a relic of the past. It is a living answer to the deepest questions of the present. It tells us who we are, why we are here, and where we are going. In a world that has lost its story, that is no small thing.

The world without God is trying to write its own meaning.

The Church exists to remind it that meaning has already been given.

That is the quiet power of faith in a secular age. Not dominance. Not control. But truth spoken with love and lived with courage. That kind of faith does not fade when the culture changes.

It shines.

Prayer

Father,

We confess how easily we drift into living as though You are distant or optional. Forgive us for the ways we have absorbed the assumptions of a world that tries to explain everything without You. Restore our sense of wonder, our reverence for truth, and our dependence on Your presence. Teach us to see reality as You see it—filled with purpose, meaning, and Your sustaining hand. Anchor our hearts in what is eternal when everything around us feels uncertain. In Jesus' name, Amen.

Reflection

1. Where in my life have I been tempted to live as though God is only a private influence rather than the center of everything?

2. What parts of modern culture have most shaped how I think about identity, purpose, or success?

3. If I am honest, do I look to God first for meaning—or to something else?

Challenge

For the next seven days, choose one daily moment to intentionally acknowledge God's presence—before work, before sleep, or before a difficult decision. Pause, pray, and remind yourself that reality is not random and life is not self-made. Let this simple act become a quiet rebellion against a world that forgets its Creator.

3

THE VANISHING OF TRUTH

Truth is not disappearing because people have become less intelligent. It is disappearing because it has become inconvenient. In an age that prizes personal freedom above all else, any claim that something is universally true feels like a threat. To say that something is right for everyone is to limit what someone else might want. And so, slowly and quietly, the idea of objective truth has been replaced with something far easier to live with: personal truth.

You can see this everywhere. People no longer ask, "Is it true?" They ask, "Is it true for me?" Belief has been redefined as preference. Conviction has been recast as intolerance. To disagree is not simply to hold a different view, but to commit a moral offense. In this new framework, truth does not unite people around reality—it divides them according to identity.

This shift did not happen overnight. It grew out of a long cultural suspicion toward anything that claimed authority. Religious claims were questioned first. Then moral claims. Then scientific ones. Eventually, even the idea that words should refer to something real began to erode. Language became fluid, and when language becomes fluid, reality soon follows.

A society that cannot agree on what is real cannot remain stable for long.

Power Replaces Reality

When truth becomes subjective, power takes its place. If there is no standard above us, then whoever controls the narrative controls reality. What is allowed to be said becomes what is allowed to be believed. What is celebrated becomes what is considered good. What is punished becomes what is considered evil. In a world without truth, there is no court of appeal—only influence.

This is why so many public conversations feel less like debates and more like trials. People are no longer trying to persuade one another. They are trying to silence one another. If there is no shared standard of truth, then winning becomes more important than understanding. The loudest voices dominate. The most organized groups prevail. And anyone who refuses to repeat the approved language is pushed to the margins.

A Clash of Two Realities

The Church was built on a very different assumption: that truth exists, that it can be known, and that it sets people free. Jesus did not say, "Your feelings will make you free." He said, "The truth will make you free." That claim alone places Christianity in direct conflict with a culture that has replaced truth with preference.

This is not a small disagreement. It is a clash between two visions of reality. One says that truth is discovered and received. The other says it is constructed and asserted. One says that reality is something we submit to. The other says it is something we invent.

Everything that follows depends on which of those visions we accept.

Once truth becomes a matter of personal preference, society begins to fracture. There is no longer a common ground where disagreements can be resolved. Each person carries their own version of reality, and when those realities collide, there is no shared standard to appeal to. What remains is not dialogue, but power—who can enforce their version of truth most effectively.

This is why institutions that once existed to seek truth now feel politicized and unstable. Universities were meant to pursue knowledge. Media was meant to report what happened. Courts were meant to weigh evidence. But when truth itself is treated as subjective, these institutions become tools for advancing narratives rather than discovering reality. Facts become flexible. Language becomes strategic. And the goal quietly shifts from understanding to influence.

People sense this, even if they cannot articulate it. They feel that something is off. They watch stories change, definitions shift, and standards move, and they grow anxious. A world where truth is always up for revision is a world where no one ever feels secure. If what is right today can be wrong tomorrow, then no one knows where they stand.

This uncertainty breeds fear, and fear breeds control. When people do not trust reality, they begin to cling to whatever group, ideology, or authority promises stability. Ironically, the rejection of objective truth does not lead to freedom. It leads to dependence. People trade the anchor of truth for the comfort of belonging, even if that belonging requires them to repeat things they know are not fully honest.

The Church has always stood in quiet opposition to this kind of world. It insists that truth is not invented by human beings but revealed by God. It insists that reality has a shape and a meaning that cannot be voted away. That claim is deeply unsettling to a culture built on self-definition, but it is also deeply liberating. When truth exists outside of us, we no longer have to carry the burden of creating it ourselves.

This is why Christianity is often accused of being rigid. It refuses to treat reality as a moving target. It speaks of right and wrong, of creation and fall, of sin and redemption, as things that are not subject to opinion. In a world that worships flexibility, that kind of clarity can feel threatening.

Yet clarity is exactly what the human soul longs for.

People do not want endless options. They want something solid to stand on. They do not want a thousand competing truths. They want one truth that holds. A culture that erases truth in the name of tolerance ends up creating confusion in the name of freedom.

And confusion never builds anything that lasts.

When Truth Vanishes, Trust Collapses

One of the quiet tragedies of a truthless age is how deeply it erodes trust. When people no longer believe that words refer to something real, every conversation becomes fragile. Promises feel empty. Commitments feel provisional. Even love begins to feel uncertain, because it is no longer anchored in anything stable. If truth is flexible, then so is everything built on it.

This is why relationships in modern culture are so easily broken. When there is no shared understanding of what is real or right, there is no foundation for perseverance. Disagreement becomes intolerable. Conflict becomes a reason to leave rather than to grow. People are encouraged to follow their truth, even when that truth contradicts the needs of others. In a world without objective truth, loyalty becomes negotiable.

The same pattern appears in public life. Leaders shift their stories. Institutions change their language. Policies are justified one way today and another way tomorrow. People stop believing what they are told, not because they are cynical, but because reality keeps being rewritten. When truth becomes unstable, trust collapses.

This creates a culture of suspicion. Everyone is watching everyone else, wondering what is being hidden or manipulated. Instead of a shared pursuit of what is real, society becomes a battlefield of competing narratives. Each group insists that its version of events is the correct one, and there is no common court of appeal to resolve the conflict.

The Church offers something profoundly different. It proclaims a God who speaks truthfully and consistently. It proclaims a Word that does not change with the seasons. It proclaims a story of creation, fall, and redemption that gives coherence to human experience. In a world where truth is always shifting, that constancy is a refuge.

Yet this is precisely what makes biblical faith uncomfortable to modern ears. A stable truth exposes unstable lives. A fixed moral order confronts fluid identities. A God who speaks authoritatively challenges a culture that wants to decide everything for itself.

The Pressure to Soften Scripture

So the pressure increases. Christians are told to soften their claims, to be less certain, to treat Scripture as a collection of inspiring ideas rather than as the revealed Word of God. Over time, some do. They trade clarity for acceptance. They trade conviction for comfort.

But a Church that surrenders truth has nothing left to offer.

If the gospel becomes just one opinion among many, it loses its power to transform. If Scripture becomes a suggestion rather than a standard, it loses its ability to guide. And if Christ becomes a personal preference rather than the Lord of reality, He loses His place at the center of life.

The vanishing of truth does not simply affect society.

It tests the Church.

The question is not whether truth will disappear from the culture.

It is whether it will disappear from the people of God.

When truth begins to fade, even conscience grows quiet. People still feel guilt, but they no longer know what to call it. They feel shame, but they are told that shame is toxic. They sense that something is wrong, yet every cultural voice insists that nothing should ever be judged. The result is not freedom—it is moral disorientation.

This is why so many people today feel both anxious and defensive. They have been told that there are no moral absolutes, yet they are constantly being evaluated by invisible standards that change without warning. One day a belief is acceptable. The next day it is condemned. Without stable truth, there can be no stable identity.

The human heart cannot live in that tension forever.

So people begin to cling to whatever gives them certainty. Some turn to political movements. Some to identity labels. Some to rigid ideologies that promise clarity in a confusing world. These systems offer a kind of moral structure, but it is a fragile one. It is based on loyalty to a group rather than on allegiance to what is real. When the group changes its mind, everyone must change with it.

This is why so many cultural debates feel so intense. They are not really about facts. They are about belonging. To disagree is to risk exile. To question is to risk being cast out. In a world without truth, social approval becomes the highest good.

The Church is called to be different.

It is called to be a people rooted in something deeper than trends or approval. It is called to bear witness to a truth that does not depend on popularity. That does not mean Christians should be cruel or dismissive. It means they must be faithful. Love without truth is sentiment. Truth without love is harshness. The gospel holds both together.

This balance is increasingly rare.

A culture that has abandoned truth cannot tell the difference between conviction and hatred. It assumes that any strong belief must be oppressive. But Scripture presents a very different picture. It shows that truth, rightly lived, is an act of love. It reveals what is real so that people can live well within it.

Truth Spoken Faithfully

To speak truth in a truthless age will always be costly. It will be misunderstood. It will be misrepresented. It will be resisted. But it will also be needed. A world drowning in confusion needs voices that are willing to speak clearly.

Not loudly.

Not angrily.

But faithfully.

One of the most damaging effects of a truthless culture is how it reshapes education. When there is no agreement about what is real, schools no longer see themselves as places that transmit knowledge. They become places that shape identity. Facts are filtered through ideology. History is rewritten through modern lenses. Science is reframed according to political priorities.

Students are not taught how to think.

They are taught what to think.

This does not produce curiosity. It produces conformity. Young people learn quickly which ideas are safe to express and which will bring consequences. They learn to perform the right beliefs, to use the approved language, and to hide any doubts that might make them stand out. Over time, the pursuit of truth gives way to the pursuit of survival.

A generation raised this way struggles to trust its own judgment.

If every authority seems compromised, and every narrative feels strategic, people stop believing that anyone is telling the truth. Cynicism becomes the default. Ironically, in a world that rejects absolute truth, manipulation becomes easier, not harder. When nothing is fixed, anything can be shaped.

The Church has often underestimated how deeply this affects young believers. They are growing up in a world where even the idea of truth has been relativized. They are told that faith is just one story among many, and that no story has the right to claim it is more real than another. Under that pressure, some quietly abandon their convictions. Others keep their faith private, unsure whether it has a place in public life.

Yet Christianity was never meant to be a private story.

It is a claim about reality itself. It declares that God exists, that He created the world, that He entered it in Christ, and that He will judge it in righteousness. These are not poetic metaphors. They are statements about what is.

This is why the gospel will always be controversial in a truthless age. It does not offer another perspective. It offers a verdict.

And a world that has learned to live without verdicts does not know what to do with one.

As truth continues to erode, even the idea of accountability begins to disappear. When no one can say with certainty what is right or wrong, responsibility becomes a burden no one wants to carry. Mistakes are reframed as misunderstandings. Sin is rebranded as self-expression. Moral failure becomes a matter of perspective rather than repentance.

This shift does not make people more compassionate. It makes them more fragile.

Without truth, people have no framework for forgiveness, because forgiveness assumes that something real went wrong. Without truth, there can be no confession, no repentance, and no restoration—only endless justification. People spend their lives defending themselves against every criticism, because there is no stable standard to appeal to. Everything becomes personal.

This is why modern culture swings so wildly between shame and defiance. One moment people are told they are perfect just the way they are. The next moment they are publicly condemned for violating invisible rules. In the absence of truth, guilt never disappears—it just becomes chaotic.

The gospel offers something radically different. It tells us that sin is real, but so is grace. It tells us that failure does not have to define us, because forgiveness is possible. It tells us that truth, when faced honestly, does not crush us—it heals us. A culture that has abandoned truth cannot offer that kind of hope.

This is why the Church must resist the temptation to soften its message. To deny sin is to deny the need for redemption. To blur truth is to empty grace of its power. The world does not need a faith that agrees with it. It needs a faith that tells it what is real and offers a way back to God.

Yet many believers feel pressure to do the opposite. They are told that clarity is cruelty and conviction is arrogance. They are encouraged to keep faith vague, to avoid hard truths, to emphasize affirmation over transformation. Over time, this produces a Church that is kind but not truthful, welcoming but not healing.

Truth is not the enemy of love.

It is the path to it.

A world that has lost truth is not liberated.

It is lost.

And the Church exists to call it home.

The cost of living in a truthless age is not only cultural; it is deeply personal. When people are taught that reality is whatever they feel it to be, they are left alone to carry the weight of their own existence. Every choice becomes a referendum on identity. Every failure becomes a verdict on worth. There is no larger story to fall back on, no higher meaning to lean into.

This is why so many people feel exhausted by life.

They are constantly trying to justify themselves, prove themselves, and protect themselves in a world where nothing is secure. Relationships become fragile. Commitments feel risky. Even faith, when reduced to personal preference, becomes another source of pressure rather than a source of peace.

The gospel offers rest in a very different way. It does not ask us to invent who we are. It tells us who we are: created, fallen, loved, and redeemable. It does not ask us to manufacture meaning. It declares that meaning has already been given. In a world obsessed with self-definition, that is a radical relief.

Yet this relief depends on truth.

If the story of God is not real, then it is just another comforting narrative. But if it is true—if Christ really lived, died, and rose again—then it changes everything. It means that reality has a center. It means that history has a direction. It means that our lives are not accidents.

This is why truth matters so much.

Without it, hope is fragile. With it, hope becomes anchored. A culture that loses truth loses more than facts. It loses the possibility of genuine joy, because joy depends on knowing that life means something beyond the moment.

The Church must remember this, even when it is pressured to forget. It must resist the temptation to trade truth for acceptance. A faith that cannot tell the truth about reality cannot offer anyone a way to live within it.

The vanishing of truth is not just a cultural crisis.

It is a spiritual one.

And the answer to it is not cleverness, but faithfulness.

The disappearance of truth does not happen all at once. It fades through small compromises, quiet silences, and the slow erosion of courage. People stop saying what they believe. Institutions stop standing for what they once knew. Over time, what was once unthinkable becomes normal, and what was once obvious becomes controversial.

Yet truth has a stubborn way of returning.

No matter how much a culture tries to bury it, reality keeps pushing back. Broken promises still hurt. Betrayal still wounds. Lies still destroy trust. Human hearts still long for something solid to stand on. The world can pretend that truth is optional, but life itself keeps exposing that it is not.

This is where the Church finds its calling again.

It does not exist to win arguments. It exists to bear witness. It does not need to shout to be heard. It needs to speak what is real and live as if it is true. In a world drowning in spin and performance, honesty becomes a form of resistance.

The truth of the gospel is not fragile. It has survived empires, persecutions, revolutions, and countless attempts to silence it. It does not depend on cultural approval. It depends on the God who revealed it. When believers cling to that truth, they become a quiet but immovable presence in a shifting world.

A culture without truth will always feel unstable.

A Church without truth will feel empty.

A Refuge for the Lost

. . .

But a Church rooted in truth becomes a refuge.

It offers something the world cannot provide: a place where reality is not negotiated, where meaning is not invented, and where hope is not a temporary illusion. In a time when everything seems up for revision, that kind of steadiness is priceless.

The vanishing of truth is not the end of the story.

It is the moment that reveals who still believes in it.

And those who do will be called to stand.

PRAYER

Father,

We live in a world that questions everything except its own assumptions. Anchor our hearts in what is true when everything feels uncertain. Give us the humility to listen, the courage to speak, and the faith to stand when truth is costly. Guard us from confusion, from fear, and from the temptation to trade conviction for comfort. Let Your Word be a lamp to our feet and a light to our path. In Jesus' name, Amen.

REFLECTION

1. Where have I been tempted to treat truth as flexible instead of foundational?

2. What voices or narratives most shape the way I see reality right now?

3. When my beliefs are challenged, do I retreat into silence or lean more deeply into God's Word?

CHALLENGE

Choose one area of your life where you've been hesitant to speak or live according to what you know is true. This week, take one deliberate step toward honesty—whether in a conversation, a decision, or a habit. Let your actions quietly reflect a confidence that truth is not something to be invented, but something to be lived.

4

THE QUIET COLLAPSE

The most dangerous moments in history rarely announce themselves with chaos. They arrive quietly, wrapped in normalcy. Institutions continue to function. Markets continue to move. People go to work, scroll their phones, raise their children, and assume tomorrow will look much like today. Meanwhile, something far more important is unraveling beneath the surface.

Civilizations do not collapse when buildings fall.

They collapse when belief erodes.

Long before laws change or borders shift, the stories a society tells itself begin to decay. The idea of what is good, what is worth protecting, and what is worth sacrificing for slowly fades. What remains may still look prosperous, but it is hollow. It no longer knows why it exists.

This is where we are now.

The signs are subtle, but they are everywhere. Families feel weaker. Communities feel thinner. Trust feels rarer. People are more connected than ever, yet lonelier than any generation before them. Anxiety and anger simmer just beneath the surface of daily life. Something essential is missing, but few can name it.

The collapse is not economic.

It is spiritual.

A culture that forgets God eventually forgets itself. It no longer remembers why human life is sacred, why truth matters, or why sacrifice is noble. Without those anchors, everything becomes negotiable. What once felt unthinkable becomes discussable. What once was immoral becomes merely controversial. What once was wrong becomes a matter of perspective.

Forgetting Before Falling

This is how decline works. It does not begin with rebellion. It begins with forgetting.

The Church is not immune to this process. When believers grow comfortable, they often stop paying attention. Faith becomes routine. Worship becomes familiar. Scripture becomes something that is known but no longer felt. Over time, vigilance fades, and spiritual drift sets in.

Yet drift is never neutral.

It always moves somewhere.

The quiet collapse is not loud enough to panic people, but it is steady enough to change everything. And unless it is recognized, it will continue.

One of the most unsettling features of cultural decline is how normal it feels while it is happening. There is no siren, no official announcement that something essential has been lost. Life simply continues, even as the foundations slowly give way. People adapt. They adjust their expectations. They lower their standards without realizing it. What once would have shocked them becomes something they quietly accept.

This is how the collapse stays quiet.

Small compromises pile up. Values that once guided decisions become optional. Truth becomes less important than convenience. Integrity becomes less important than comfort. And over time, the moral compass of a society drifts off course.

The same thing happens in individual lives. People rarely wake up one morning and decide to abandon what they believe. They simply make small choices that move them away from it. They skip prayer. They soften a conviction. They avoid a difficult conversation. They tell themselves it does not really matter. But small choices, repeated over time, create a new direction. *Drift always feels harmless in the moment.*

Yet Scripture warns that neglect is often more dangerous than open rebellion. When people forget what they once knew, they do not notice what they are losing. Faith fades not because it is attacked, but because it is ignored. And a faith that is ignored will not survive long.

This is why spiritual apathy is so deadly. It lulls people into thinking everything is fine while something vital is being drained away. Churches still meet. Songs are still sung. But the fire that once burned at the center begins to dim. Without vigilance, what remains is a shell.

The quiet collapse is not dramatic, but it is relentless. It moves through homes, schools, and churches alike. It thrives on distraction. It feeds on comfort. And it advances whenever people stop asking whether they are still faithful. *Recognizing it is the first act of resistance.*

Distracted Into Weakness

One of the greatest tools of spiritual erosion is distraction. It does not confront belief; it simply overwhelms it. People are not persuaded to stop caring about what matters most. They are given so many things to care about that they have no space left for what matters at all. Noise replaces reflection. Busyness replaces devotion. And slowly, the soul grows thin.

This is not an accident.

Modern life is designed to keep people constantly occupied. Screens demand attention. Notifications interrupt thought. Entertainment fills every quiet moment. A distracted mind rarely asks deep questions. A distracted heart rarely notices its own emptiness. In a culture of endless stimulation, spiritual hunger is easily buried.

Yet buried is not the same as gone.

Beneath the noise, people still feel restless. They still sense that something is missing. They just do not know how to name it. Instead of turning inward or upward, they reach for the next distraction. The cycle continues.

The Church has often underestimated how powerful this force is. Distraction makes faith shallow. It turns prayer into something rushed, Scripture into something skimmed, and worship into something consumed rather than offered. Over time, believers begin to know less about what they believe and feel less connected to why they believe it. *A distracted faith cannot withstand pressure.*

When trials come, or when culture pushes back, a shallow faith collapses. It has no roots. It has no depth. It has never learned to be still long enough to hear God's voice.

The quiet collapse thrives on this. It does not need to attack the Church directly. It only needs to keep it busy.

When Fear Replaces Trust

As distraction weakens spiritual depth, fear begins to take its place. When people are no longer anchored in something eternal, they become increasingly sensitive to threats, real or imagined. Their sense of security shifts from God to circumstances. They begin to measure safety by comfort, stability, and approval.

This is how fear quietly reshapes faith.

Believers who once trusted God in hardship begin to seek control instead. They avoid difficult truths. They hesitate to speak. They retreat into silence when conviction would cost them something. Fear does not announce itself loudly. It whispers caution. It urges compromise. It tells people that peace is more important than faithfulness.

Over time, this creates a Church that is polite but powerless.

People still gather. They still sing. They still pray. But they have lost the confidence that God is bigger than their circumstances. When faith becomes cautious, it stops being courageous. When it stops being courageous, it stops being influential.

The quiet collapse does not remove Christianity from society. It removes its boldness. A Church that is afraid of offending is easily controlled. A Church that fears rejection is easily manipulated. The gospel becomes something to be managed rather than proclaimed.

Yet Scripture is filled with stories of people who stood when standing was dangerous. Their faith was not based on safety. It was based on trust. They knew that obedience mattered more than survival.

The quiet collapse happens when that trust fades.

Another sign of quiet collapse is how easily truth is softened in the name of unity. Unity is a beautiful thing when it is built on shared conviction. It becomes dangerous when it is built on shared avoidance. Churches begin to avoid difficult passages of Scripture. Leaders learn which topics make people uncomfortable. Conversations become carefully managed. What is left unsaid begins to matter more than what is spoken. *This creates a culture of spiritual politeness.*

No one wants to be the one who disrupts the mood. No one wants to be labeled divisive. So clarity is traded for harmony, and conviction is traded for consensus. Over time, the sharp edges of the gospel are dulled. Sin is discussed in vague terms. Repentance is rarely called for. Grace is celebrated, but the truth that gives grace its meaning is quietly set aside.

Yet a unity that requires silence is not unity at all.

It is avoidance.

The gospel was never designed to make everyone comfortable. It was designed to make people free. That freedom comes through truth, and truth often creates tension before it creates healing. A Church that refuses to allow tension will also refuse to allow transformation.

The quiet collapse thrives in these conditions. It does not need to destroy belief. It only needs to make it optional. When faith becomes something that must never challenge, it stops being something that can change.

Real unity is forged in shared surrender to truth, not in shared denial of it.

Perhaps the most subtle danger of all is how success can mask spiritual decline. Churches can grow. Platforms can expand. Programs can multiply. Yet something essential can still be missing. Numbers can rise while depth falls. Applause can increase while conviction fades. A culture that measures everything by visible results will often mistake activity for faithfulness. *The quiet collapse hides behind achievement.*

When outward success becomes the primary goal, inward surrender becomes negotiable. Leaders feel pressure to keep people happy. Messages are shaped to avoid offense. Hard truths are postponed for a more convenient time that never comes. What remains looks healthy, but it lacks the power to withstand hardship.

This is why trials reveal so much. When comfort disappears, shallow faith collapses. When cultural approval fades, borrowed conviction evaporates. What is left is what was truly there all along.

The Church was never called to be impressive.

It was called to be faithful.

Faithfulness is quieter than popularity, but it is far stronger. It does not depend on trends or approval. It does not bend when circumstances change. It remains rooted when everything else shakes.

The quiet collapse advances wherever faith is replaced by performance. It moves in when appearances matter more than obedience. It thrives when the Church begins to mirror the culture instead of calling it to something higher.

Yet even now, God is at work.

He is awakening hearts that have grown dull. He is stirring consciences that have been lulled by comfort. He is calling people back to what is real. The quiet collapse is not the end of the story. It is the moment before a choice.

And that choice still matters.

Awakening Before It's Too Late

Every generation is eventually confronted with a moment of reckoning. The habits that once seemed harmless are exposed. The compromises that once felt small reveal their true cost. People begin to sense that something precious has been lost, even if they cannot fully explain what it was.

This is the moment many believers are living in now.

They feel the thinness of modern faith. They sense the absence of depth. They notice how easily Scripture is sidelined and how quickly prayer is forgotten. They recognize that something vital has been traded away, but they are not always sure how it happened.

The answer is simple, though not easy: it happened through neglect.

Faith is not something that survives on autopilot. It must be tended, nourished, and protected. When it is not, it does not explode—it fades. It becomes quieter, weaker, easier to ignore. Over time, what was once central becomes peripheral.

Yet awareness changes everything.

When people finally realize what has been happening, they are given a chance to respond. They can continue drifting, or they can turn back. They can accept the quiet collapse, or they can resist it.

Resistance does not begin with grand gestures.

It begins with repentance.

It begins when people return to prayer, to Scripture, to honest community. It begins when they decide that comfort is not worth the cost of compromise. It begins when they choose faithfulness over familiarity.

The quiet collapse only wins when no one notices.

But many are noticing now.

The quiet collapse does not have the final word. It reveals the weakness of what was built on comfort, but it also exposes the strength of what is built on truth. When superficial faith begins to fall away, what remains is something far more valuable: a people who know why they believe. *This is where renewal begins*

Not with noise, not with spectacle, but with conviction. When believers rediscover the weight of Scripture, the power of prayer, and the cost of obedience, something shifts. Faith stops being a habit and becomes a commitment again. The gospel stops being a message we hear and becomes a reality we live.

God has always worked this way. He allows what is shallow to be shaken so that what is rooted can stand. He allows decline to reveal what was never truly alive. And then, in that honesty, He begins to rebuild.

The quiet collapse is painful, but it is also merciful. It strips away illusions. It removes false security. It calls people back to what is real.

The Church does not need to be rescued from this moment.

It needs to be refined by it.

A people who have been awakened to what has been lost are far more powerful than a people who never noticed. They will pray with urgency. They will live with intention. They will stand with courage. They will no longer mistake comfort for faith.

The quiet collapse has already begun.

So has the awakening.

PRAYER

Father,

We confess how easily we drift when life becomes comfortable and faith becomes familiar. Wake us from spiritual sleep. Restore in us a hunger for Your Word, a passion for Your presence, and a courage that does not depend on approval. Where we have grown careless, make us attentive. Where we have grown afraid, make us bold. Do not let us mistake activity for faithfulness or comfort for truth. In Jesus' name, Amen.

REFLECTION

1. Where in my spiritual life have I noticed drift or complacency?

2. What habits or distractions have slowly crowded out prayer, Scripture, or obedience?

3. If I am honest, what would it look like for me to take my faith more seriously right now?

CHALLENGE

Choose one daily practice you have neglected—prayer, Scripture, silence, or fellowship—and commit to restoring it for the next seven days. Set a time. Protect it. Let it be a deliberate step away from drift and toward renewal. The quiet collapse is resisted one faithful choice at a time.

5

THE COST OF CLARITY

"If we stay vague on the hard truths, maybe we can keep everyone happy."

That dangerous lie has seeped into many hearts today. It promises a cheap peace—comfort without conviction, relationship without repentance. But the peace of ambiguity is a fragile illusion. Every time the church mutes a clear truth to avoid offense, something vital is lost. Every retreat into vagueness costs reality in souls and in integrity. The cost of clarity may be high, but the cost of avoiding clarity is far higher. We are living through the bill coming due.

Clarity of belief, values, and doctrine was once a hallmark of vibrant faith. Now it's often seen as arrogance or extremism. In a culture that glorifies confusion, drawing a clear line is the one unforgivable sin. Say plainly that Jesus is the only way, and you're labeled intolerant. Affirm the sacredness of life or the created boundaries of male and female, and you may be called hateful or backward. Stand on Scripture's authority, and you'll be mocked as ignorant or fanatical. The world around us is happy with Christianity as long as it stays blurry. The moment it comes into focus—definite and unapologetic—pressure mounts. Suddenly friends distance themselves. Employers question your "fit." Social media piles on. The message is clear: Clarity is unwelcome.

Why Clarity Is Unwelcome

Why does clarity provoke such backlash? Because clarity shines a light, and light always exposes. A confused culture finds comfort in the shadows of uncertainty. If all truth is relative, no one is ever wrong, and no change is ever demanded. But a clear voice saying, "This is true and that is false," upsets that false peace. It forces a choice. When the early church proclaimed "Jesus is Lord"—and not Caesar—they weren't just making a religious statement. They were drawing a line in a world that preferred its truths mixed and malleable. And they paid dearly for it. Their clarity about Christ's lordship cost them reputation, rights, and often their very lives. They had no social status to shield, no political power to protect. What they had was conviction, and conviction was enough to turn the world upside down.

Today we face a different empire of confusion, but the tension remains the same. Our society preaches, "Believe whatever you want—just don't claim it's the truth." It celebrates those who say "maybe" and scorns those who say "definitely." In this environment, the temptation to soften our stance is strong. It is so much easier to trade conviction for comfort, to tell ourselves we're being "loving" by staying silent. Who doesn't want to avoid the friction, to sidestep the awkward conversations and the angry labels? Silence is easier in the moment. Going along does feel safer. Even within our own hearts, there's a subtle relief in not having to take a firm stand.

Yet every time we choose comfort over clarity, something within us erodes. The silence leaves a hollow echo. We know we were made for more than polite appeasement. We sense that a love without truth isn't real love at all. Jesus never once chose comfortable ambiguity over hard clarity—and He loved people more deeply than we ever will. He warned that following Him would bring a sword of division, cutting even between family members. He knew what we forget: real peace is the fruit of truth, not the avoidance of it. Conviction and comfort rarely ride together. We will ultimately choose one as our guide.

What Clarity Will Cost

Clarity will cost us. There's no pretending otherwise. If we decide to live and speak with clear conviction in this confused age, we will pay a price in at least three currencies: social, personal, and spiritual. Socially, clarity can cost us popularity and place. You might lose friendships when you don't join in the latest ideological fad. You might be marginalized at work for refusing to celebrate what God calls sin. In some places, you risk your freedom or safety by simply speaking biblical truth in public. Personally, clarity will cost our comfort and pride. Taking a stand often feels lonely. It isolates you as "the unreasonable one," "the rigid one," "the fanatic." It can stir up self-doubt in the lonely midnight hour: "Wouldn't life be simpler if I just kept quiet?" Your heart will ache as you count the opportunities and honors you forfeited because you wouldn't compromise. And spiritually, clarity will draw the enemy's attention. Make no mistake: Satan is quite content with a muddled, lukewarm church. But the moment a believer resolves to speak truth plainly, all hell seems to mobilize. Temptations to quit intensify. Doubts cloud the mind. The enemy whispers that you're doing more harm than good, that your courage is pride or your sacrifice is foolish.

These costs are real, and they hurt. Jobs lost. Friendships ended. Families divided. Reputations smeared. Comforts forfeited. We need to acknowledge that pain. It is okay to feel the weight of it; even Jesus in Gethsemane sweat drops of blood facing the cost of His mission. But He also showed us what to do with that weight: He entrusted it to the Father's will. In our far smaller trials, we too can entrust our losses to God. He sees every sacrifice made for the sake of truth. Not one tear shed for Christ is wasted.

Clarity demands courage, yes, but not a courage we must manufacture on our own. It is a courage fueled by love—love for God and love for others. Why face these costs at all? Why not slip back into the soothing waters of ambiguity and spare ourselves? Because clarity is an act of love. To speak the truth that sets people free is the purest love, even if it's received as hate. To refuse to lie about what will destroy someone's soul is to truly care for them. The world has enough people pandering and patronizing; it is starving for those willing to lovingly say, "This is the way—walk in it."

And clarity is also an act of worship. When we hold fast to sound doctrine and godly values in a confused age, we declare that God's truth is worth more to us than the approval of men. Every time you choose conviction over compromise, heaven rejoices at a believer who values God above all. In those moments, you are standing in a great and noble tradition—the "cloud of witnesses" who chose the same. Think of Daniel's three friends refusing to blur the line before Nebuchadnezzar's idol. Clarity put them in a fiery furnace, but also into the company of the Fourth Man who met them there. Think of Martin Luther standing before the empire's diet, refusing to recant the clear gospel he'd found in Scripture, saying, "Here I stand, I can do no other." History is made by men and women who paid the price of clarity with their comfort, and changed the world in the process.

Now it is our turn. By God's strange design, we have been placed in a generation awash with uncertainty, where even the definitions of male and female, truth and lie, love and hate change by the week. Into this sea of confusion, God calls His people to be anchors of clarity. Not abrasive or obnoxious, but unflinching and unmistakable. The call will not be without cost. The fog of relativism will swirl around us, trying to obscure the way. The cultural winds will blow against us, urging us to drift along. Many will not understand why we won't "get with the times." Some will accuse us of pride for daring to be sure of anything. Others will hate us simply because we refuse to call darkness light. But by the grace of God, we can withstand all of it—not with harshness or self-righteousness, but with quiet, steady resolve grounded in something (or rather Someone) eternal.

Choosing Conviction Over Comfort

This is the tension we must live in: conviction or comfort, clarity or compromise. We cannot have both. If we choose comfort, we may avoid some conflict for a time, but we'll also avoid growth, holiness, and impact. The gospel cannot shine through a muddy lens. Sooner or later, a church that will not speak clearly ceases to speak at all. On the other hand, if we choose conviction—if we embrace the discomfort and the consequences—it will be hard. There will be days when we wonder if it's worth it. But those are the days heaven leans in close and the Spirit whispers, "Take heart... for great is your reward." Those are the moments that forge a faith deep and unshakeable, refined like gold in a fire.

So we set our eyes on Jesus, the one who perfectly embodied grace and truth. He is the one who stood before rulers and councils, never wavering about who He was or why He came. He is the one who could have called legions of angels to avoid the cross, but instead chose clarity—openly confessing His kingship—knowing it would cost His life. He is the author and finisher of our faith, and He gives us the courage to follow in His footsteps when clarity costs us dearly.

Will we follow Him there? This is the question that confronts every believer in every generation, but especially ours. In an age that feasts on ambiguity, will we have the courage to speak plainly? When the pressure hits—when the heat of criticism or the chill of exclusion bears down—will we still stand in the open and say, "Here I stand, I can do no other"? The journey of the faithful has never been one of ease, and ours is no exception. But clarity of faith and truth has always been the spark that ignites revival and the stake upon which renewal is won. The world may not welcome our clarity, but it desperately needs it.

Let Part 1 of this chapter settle that challenge in our hearts. Take a moment and consider: Where have I settled for comfort over conviction? Where has fear of conflict kept me silent when I should have spoken? These questions aren't meant to condemn us, but to awaken us. We all have felt that fear and that pull to blend in. But God is calling us higher, to a holy boldness wrapped in love. In the next part, we will delve deeper into what it means to pay the price of clarity with faith and hope. For now, it's enough to feel the weight of the call and the cost: to let it drive us to prayer, to reflection, and ultimately to a decision.

Clarity will cost us in this life—of that there is no doubt. But as we will continue to see, it is in paying that price that we find out what our faith is truly worth. And if we listen closely, beyond the clamor of a confused world, we can hear the promise that makes it all worthwhile: "Blessed are you when people insult you, persecute you, and falsely say all kinds of evil against you because of Me... Rejoice and be glad, because great is your reward in heaven." The cost of clarity is real, but so is the reward. The question now before each of us is simply this: Is the Truth worth that cost?

Clarity does not just cost us externally. It also costs us internally. There is a price paid in the private places of the heart long before it is ever paid in public. Choosing conviction over comfort means confronting our own fears, our own desire to be liked, and our own reluctance to stand alone. It means admitting that part of us would rather blend in than be set apart.

No one is immune to that tension.

Every believer, at some point, feels the pull to soften what they believe. To round off the sharp edges. To say less than they know is true so that life will feel easier. That temptation does not come from a lack of faith—it comes from being human. We were created for relationship, for belonging, for acceptance. The pain of being misunderstood or rejected cuts deep.

But truth has never been maintained by those who felt no fear.

It has always been preserved by those who acted in spite of it.

The apostles knew what it meant to be ostracized. They were beaten, imprisoned, and killed not because they were hateful, but because they were clear. They would not stop saying that Jesus is Lord. They would not stop proclaiming that repentance leads to life. Their clarity made them dangerous to a world built on lies.

That same dynamic still exists.

A culture that is invested in confusion will always resist those who bring clarity. Lies require silence to survive. Deception needs people to look the other way. The moment someone stands up and says, "This is not true," the illusion begins to crack. That is why courage is contagious—and why it is so often targeted.

Yet clarity is not about winning arguments.

It is about being faithful to what is real.

We do not speak the truth because it guarantees success. We speak it because it is right. Obedience is not measured by outcomes but by alignment. When we live in step with truth, we are walking with God, even if the world walks away.

This is where many believers become exhausted. They want to see results. They want to feel that their stand is making a difference. When change does not come quickly, or when opposition increases, discouragement sets in. It is tempting to think that clarity is pointless when it seems to produce only conflict.

But conflict is not failure.

It is often the first sign that truth has been heard.

The gospel has always been a dividing line. Not because it seeks division, but because it exposes what is hidden. Light does not create darkness—it reveals it. When clarity enters a space, whatever is built on falsehood begins to react. That reaction is not a reason to retreat. It is evidence that something real is happening.

We must also remember that clarity is not the same as cruelty. Speaking truth does not require harshness. It requires honesty wrapped in love. Jesus did not hesitate to confront sin, but He did so with compassion for the sinner. His clarity did not come from anger. It came from deep, unshakeable love for what is true and for those who were being destroyed by lies.

That is the spirit we are called to carry.

The cost of clarity will never be paid all at once. It is paid daily, in small decisions: whether to stay silent or speak, whether to blend in or stand out, whether to choose comfort or conviction. Each choice shapes who we become.

And over time, those choices reveal what we truly believe.

The true measure of clarity is not how loudly we speak, but how faithfully we live. Words can be easy; consistency is not. To stand in truth day after day, especially when it brings discomfort, requires a kind of endurance that only deep conviction can sustain. Anyone can be bold for a moment. It takes faith to remain clear over a lifetime. *This is where many believers quietly falter.*

They may agree with truth in principle, but they hesitate to let it shape their choices. They know what Scripture says, yet they delay obedience because it feels costly. They tell themselves there will be a better time, a safer moment, a less complicated situation. But clarity postponed is clarity denied. A truth we refuse to live is a truth we no longer fully believe.

Jesus never offered His followers an easy path. He offered them a narrow one. He warned that those who walk it would be misunderstood, opposed, and sometimes hated. Yet He also promised that those who lose their lives for His sake will find them. The cost of clarity is not paid without reward. It is paid with the promise of a deeper, truer life.

A faith that avoids discomfort becomes fragile.

A faith that endures it becomes strong.

This is why God often allows His people to be placed in difficult, uncertain, or even hostile environments. It is there that clarity is tested. When belief is no longer convenient, it must either deepen or disappear. Trials refine conviction. Pressure exposes what is real.

And what is real will stand.

The world is not confused about everything. It is confused about what matters most. In that confusion, the Church is called to be a steady presence. Not aggressive. Not afraid. Just clear. Clear about who God is. Clear about what He has said. Clear about what it means to live in His truth.

That clarity will never make everyone comfortable.

But it will always make faith real.

As this chapter closes, the question remains simple and unavoidable:

Will we be people who know the truth but hide it, or people who know the truth and live it?

The cost of clarity is real.

So is its power.

PRAYER

Father,

Give us the courage to live what we believe, even when it is costly. Strengthen our hearts when fear whispers that silence is safer than truth. Teach us to trust You more than the approval of others and to value obedience more than comfort. Let our lives be marked by clarity, not compromise, and by faith, not fear. In Jesus' name, Amen.

REFLECTION

1. Where have I felt pressure to soften or hide what I truly believe?

2. What truths have I delayed living because they feel uncomfortable or risky?

3. How might God be calling me to be more clear and courageous right now?

CHALLENGE

Identify one area where you have been hesitant to stand for what is right. This week, take one deliberate step—small or large—toward living with greater clarity. Let it be a reminder that faith grows stronger when it is exercised, not when it is hidden.

6

WHEN FAITH BECOMES QUIET

There is a moment in every believer's life when faith stops being something we talk about and becomes something we are tempted to hide. It does not happen because we suddenly stop believing. It happens because belief begins to feel inconvenient. The room grows colder. The looks grow sharper. The cost of honesty becomes clearer. And quietly, almost without noticing, we learn how to stay silent.

This is how faith becomes quiet.

It is not usually silenced by persecution. It is muted by social pressure. People learn which words make others uncomfortable. They learn which convictions invite ridicule. They learn which Scriptures sound too exclusive, too old-fashioned, too certain. And so they adjust. They soften their language. They change the subject. They tell themselves they are being wise.

But wisdom that is built on fear is not wisdom at all.

The early Christians lived under real threat. They could lose their freedom, their livelihoods, even their lives for refusing to deny Christ. Yet it was not fear that defined them. It was clarity. They did not shout, but they did not hide. They spoke what they knew to be true, even when it cost them everything.

We face a different kind of pressure today, but it is no less powerful. Our culture punishes clarity not with prisons, but with shame. Not with chains, but with labels. People are not dragged away—they are dismissed, mocked, sidelined, or digitally erased. The result is the same: silence. This silence spreads.

When one believer stops speaking, others notice. They take note of what happens to those who stand out. Slowly, a culture of quiet settles in. Faith becomes something that is kept inside, never expressed too strongly. Christianity becomes something that is personal but not public, private but not visible.

Yet a faith that cannot be seen cannot change anything.

Jesus never told His followers to keep their light hidden. He warned that hiding it defeats its purpose. Light exists to be seen. Truth exists to be spoken. When the Church grows quiet, the world does not become more peaceful. It becomes more lost.

The question before us is not whether pressure will come.

It already has.

The question is whether we will let that pressure define us, or whether we will let truth do it instead.

How Faith Learns to Be Quiet

Silence often feels safer than truth. When we speak clearly about what we believe, we risk being misunderstood. We risk being labeled. We risk losing relationships, opportunities, or approval. So we begin to tell ourselves that staying quiet is simply being kind, that not saying anything is a form of peacekeeping.

But silence has consequences.

When believers stop speaking, other voices rush in to fill the space. Ideas that once would have been questioned become normal. Lies that once would have been challenged become accepted. A quiet Church does not stop the world from moving—it simply stops guiding where it goes.

This is why cultural shifts feel so sudden. They are not sudden at all. They happen slowly, as fewer and fewer people are willing to say, "This is not true." What was once unthinkable becomes discussable. What was once controversial becomes common. And eventually, what was once wrong becomes celebrated.

Faith does not disappear all at once.

It fades when it is no longer voiced.

Yet Scripture reminds us that confession is part of belief. To believe something deeply is to speak it openly. Faith that is never expressed eventually weakens. Like a muscle that is never used, it loses its strength.

The question is not whether we have faith in our hearts.

It is whether we have the courage to let it be heard.

There is a difference between wisdom and fear, but in a pressured culture the two are often confused. Wisdom knows when to speak and when to be silent. Fear wants silence all the time. It convinces us that any expression of conviction is dangerous, that any clear statement of belief will cause harm.

Fear always exaggerates the cost of faithfulness.

It tells us that one honest word will ruin everything, that one firm stand will destroy every relationship. But more often than not, what fear really protects is our comfort. It wants to preserve our image, our ease, and our sense of belonging, even if it means shrinking our witness.

Jesus never told His followers to be reckless. But He did tell them to be courageous. Courage does not mean saying everything that comes to mind. It means refusing to deny what we know to be true. There is a world of difference between being harsh and being honest.

The Church loses its voice not when it is persecuted, but when it is afraid.

And fear is contagious.

When leaders grow cautious, communities follow. When conviction is hidden at the top, it becomes invisible at the bottom. Over time, faith becomes something people still feel, but no longer trust enough to express.

Yet God has never worked through a quiet, fearful people.

When faith grows quiet, it does not only affect what we say—it affects what we believe we are allowed to believe. Silence begins to reshape conviction. Over time, people start to doubt truths they once held with confidence, not because those truths changed, but because they no longer hear them spoken.

What we do not voice, we slowly begin to question.

This is why community matters so much in the life of faith. Belief was never meant to be carried alone. It is strengthened when it is shared. It grows when it is spoken, sung, prayed, and confessed together. A Church that stops affirming what it believes will eventually forget what it believes.

The quiet collapse of faith often begins in these small absences. Fewer testimonies. Fewer prayers spoken aloud. Fewer conversations about God outside of safe, controlled spaces. The language of faith becomes thin. What remains is habit without heat.

Yet God designed His people to be a living witness. The early believers did not merely hold truth privately; they declared it publicly. They sang it in prison cells. They prayed it in public squares. They lived it in hostile cities. Their courage did not come from having no fear—it came from having something more powerful than fear.

Silence has a way of shrinking faith.

Speech has a way of strengthening it.

One of the most painful effects of a quiet faith is how it isolates believers from one another. When no one speaks openly about what they believe, everyone begins to feel alone in their convictions. People assume they are the only ones who still care deeply, the only ones who still struggle, the only ones who still wrestle with doubt and hope. Silence creates loneliness.

This is one of the enemy's most effective strategies. He does not need to convince believers to abandon their faith. He only needs to convince them that they are alone in it. Once that lie takes root, discouragement follows. People grow weary. They begin to wonder if it is worth holding on when no one else seems to be standing.

But the truth is very different.

There are always more people who believe than it appears. They are simply quiet. They are waiting for someone else to speak first. When one voice breaks the silence, others often find the courage to join. Clarity is contagious. So is courage.

This is why even a single honest confession of faith can have a ripple effect. One prayer spoken aloud. One conviction shared gently. One truth stated without apology. These small acts of openness remind others that they are not alone.

And in that reminder, faith begins to breathe again.

Finding Our Voice Again

When believers begin to find their voice again, something shifts inside them. Faith that is spoken grows stronger. Conviction that is shared becomes steadier. What once felt fragile begins to feel firm. This is not because the world becomes more accepting, but because the heart becomes more anchored.

Speaking truth out loud has a way of clarifying what we actually believe.

Many people do not realize how much they doubt until they try to articulate their faith. Words force us to be honest. They reveal where our confidence is real and where it is thin. This is not something to fear. It is an invitation to grow.

God often uses confession as a tool of transformation.

When we name what we believe, we step into it more fully. When we say, "I trust God," we are reminded that trust is not just an idea—it is a commitment. When we say, "I follow Christ," we are declaring that our loyalty is not to the crowd, but to Him.

A quiet faith can survive.

A spoken faith can thrive.

This is why worship, prayer, and testimony are so powerful. They take what is inside and bring it into the open. They align the heart with the mouth and the life. They create coherence between what we believe and how we live.

The world may not celebrate this kind of clarity.

But the soul depends on it.

There comes a moment when every believer must decide whether faith will remain a private comfort or become a public commitment. Private faith is safe. It requires nothing. It never risks rejection. But it also never changes anything. Public faith, on the other hand, invites both connection and conflict. It exposes us to misunderstanding, but it also allows us to be truly known.

Jesus never invited people into a secret discipleship.

He called them openly. He walked with them publicly. He asked them to follow Him in ways that others could see. Faith was never meant to be invisible. It was meant to be a witness.

This does not mean every believer must be loud. It means every believer must be real. Quiet conviction that is lived with integrity is just as powerful as bold proclamation. What matters is not volume, but authenticity. When our lives align with what we claim to believe, our faith speaks even when our mouths are closed.

Yet there are moments when silence is not an option.

There are times when truth must be spoken because love demands it. When injustice must be named. When lies must be challenged. When hope must be offered. In those moments, a quiet faith is not enough.

The world does not need more hidden believers.

It needs visible ones.

The silence of believers has never changed the world. It has only allowed the world to drift further from truth. But when faith is lived openly—whether in gentle courage or bold conviction—it becomes a light that others can see. Not everyone will welcome it, but many will be drawn to it.

People are not only confused.

They are searching.

They are looking for something solid in a culture that keeps shifting. They are listening for a voice that speaks with clarity and compassion. When believers find their voice again, even in small ways, they offer that stability. They remind others that there is something worth standing on.

Faith does not have to shout to be heard.

It simply has to be present.

A Church that is willing to be seen—imperfect, honest, and faithful—will always matter more than one that stays safely hidden. The quiet of fear can be broken. The stillness of courage can take its place.

And when it does, faith begins to sound like hope again.

PRAYER

. . .

Father,

Forgive us for the times we have hidden our faith when we should have lived it. Give us courage that is gentle, boldness that is humble, and voices that speak truth with love. Where fear has made us silent, restore our confidence in You. Teach us to trust You more than our comfort and to follow You more than the crowd. In Jesus' name, Amen.

REFLECTION

1. Where in my life has faith become quiet out of fear or convenience?

2. What truth have I been hesitant to speak or live openly?

3. How might God be inviting me to let my faith be seen again?

CHALLENGE

This week, take one small step to let your faith be visible—through a conversation, an act of kindness, or a simple expression of what you believe. Let it be gentle, but let it be real. Even a quiet light can guide someone who is lost.

7

THE COST OF STANDING

Most people do not abandon truth because they hate it — they abandon it because it becomes inconvenient. In every generation, there is a moment when believing the right thing begins to cost something. That is when faith is no longer theoretical. It becomes real when it demands courage instead of comfort. Our culture has reached that moment. Christianity is no longer applauded by society; it is increasingly tolerated at best and resisted at worst. And in that shift, many believers are discovering that conviction carries a price they were never taught to expect.

For decades, faith existed in a cultural environment that made it easy to belong. Churches were respected, Christian language was familiar, and moral assumptions still loosely reflected biblical principles. But that world is fading. We now live in a society that defines truth by feelings, morality by consensus, and identity by self-creation. In such a world, Christianity is no longer neutral — it is disruptive. To claim that God defines truth, right and wrong, and human purpose is to stand against the very foundation of modern culture.

That is why the pressure on believers is increasing. It does not always come through persecution or laws. More often, it comes through social and emotional pressure — the quiet suggestion that if you truly loved people, you would remain silent. But silence is not love when truth is at stake. Love without truth becomes sentimentality, and sentimentality cannot save anyone. To follow Christ has always meant being willing to stand when standing is difficult, and to speak when speaking is costly.

What is being tested in this moment is not whether people call themselves Christians, but whether they are willing to live as if Jesus actually reigns. A faith that only exists when it is popular is not faith at all. It is a performance. The real question is whether we believe Christ is worth the price of being misunderstood, criticized, or even rejected.

The Pressure to Conform

Every culture creates boundaries around what is acceptable to believe, and those boundaries are enforced not only by laws but by shame. In our time, the greatest threat to faith is not violence but social exile. People are taught that disagreement is cruelty and that conviction is hatred. As a result, many believers begin to soften their language, blur their beliefs, and retreat from difficult truths in order to avoid being labeled or rejected. What begins as a desire to be kind slowly becomes a refusal to be honest.

This pressure is subtle but powerful. It works by convincing Christians that they can follow Jesus privately while surrendering His authority publicly. Faith is allowed as long as it remains invisible. You may pray, but you must not speak. You may believe, but you must not challenge. You may worship, but you must not assert that Christ has authority over culture, morality, or truth. In this way, Christianity is slowly reduced to a harmless hobby rather than a living allegiance.

But Jesus never offered that kind of faith. He did not ask His followers to admire Him quietly; He asked them to follow Him openly. To belong to Christ has always meant being willing to be seen, known, and sometimes opposed. The cross was never a symbol of safety — it was a declaration of surrender. And anyone who claims to follow a crucified Savior must expect that the world will eventually resist them.

This does not mean believers are called to be hostile or aggressive. It means they are called to be faithful. Faithfulness is not measured by how well we blend in but by how firmly we remain when the world pushes back. In an age that demands conformity, even quiet integrity becomes a form of courage.

The Inner Cost

The greatest cost of standing for truth is not always paid in public. It is often paid in the private places of the heart. It is paid when we choose integrity over approval, obedience over ease, and faithfulness over belonging. Every time we refuse to compromise, we feel the quiet weight of what it would have cost us to give in — fewer conflicts, smoother relationships, greater comfort. But what we gain in those moments is something far more valuable: a clear conscience and a steady soul.

Many believers underestimate how deeply fear can shape their choices. We may still believe the right things, but we hesitate to live them out when the social cost feels too high. We delay difficult conversations. We avoid uncomfortable truths. We stay silent when we should speak. Over time, this creates a quiet erosion of confidence. A faith that is never tested eventually begins to feel fragile, because it has never been proven.

Yet Scripture shows us that faith grows strongest under pressure. When conviction is challenged, it is refined. When belief is opposed, it is clarified. The early Christians did not become bold by living in safety; they became bold by facing risk. Their courage was not the absence of fear — it was the decision to obey God in spite of it. That same choice confronts believers today, even if the dangers now come through rejection instead of imprisonment.

To stand for truth in this moment requires more than agreement. It requires resolve. It means deciding in advance that obedience is worth whatever it costs. When that decision is made, fear loses much of its power. We may still feel it, but it no longer controls us. A heart anchored in truth can endure what a heart anchored in approval cannot.

What Is Really at Stake

When believers hesitate to stand, it is rarely because they do not know what is right. It is because they fear what will happen if they act on it. The stakes feel personal. Friendships may change. Careers may be affected. Family relationships may become strained. In a world that punishes dissent, standing for truth can feel like stepping into isolation. But what is truly at stake is not merely what we might lose — it is who we become.

Every compromise shapes the soul. Each time we choose silence over honesty, something inside us weakens. We may avoid conflict, but we also lose clarity. Over time, the distance between what we believe and how we live grows wider, and that distance creates a quiet kind of despair. Integrity is not just a moral ideal; it is a source of spiritual health. Without it, faith becomes exhausting rather than life-giving.

This is why Jesus spoke so often about counting the cost. He knew that discipleship would not always be rewarded with comfort. He knew that allegiance to Him would sometimes place people at odds with their own communities. But He also knew that a life built on truth is stronger than a life built on acceptance. The momentary pain of standing is always outweighed by the lasting peace of knowing you did what was right.

The world may never celebrate faithfulness, but heaven always does. And in the end, it is heaven's approval that matters most.

Standing Without Becoming Hard

One of the greatest fears many believers have is that standing for truth will make them cold, judgmental, or harsh. They worry that conviction will turn into arrogance and that clarity will turn into cruelty. This fear is understandable, because history has seen moments when truth was spoken without love. But the solution to misuse of truth is not silence — it is maturity.

Jesus never compromised truth, yet He was never cruel. He confronted sin, but He did so with compassion. He drew clear lines, but He also welcomed broken people. Real courage does not harden the heart. It deepens it. When truth is carried with humility, it becomes healing instead of wounding.

Standing for what is right does not mean standing against people. It means standing for what leads to life. A believer who speaks with grace, patience, and respect can hold firm convictions without becoming rigid or hostile. This is not weakness — it is strength under control. It takes far more courage to speak truth gently than to shout it in anger.

In a culture that equates disagreement with hatred, Christians must learn to stand in a way that reflects the character of Christ. Firm but kind. Clear but compassionate. Unmoved by pressure, yet never unmoved by love. When truth is lived this way, it becomes difficult to dismiss, even when it is resisted.

. . .

The Witness of a Steady Life

One of the most powerful forms of courage is consistency. In a world that constantly shifts, a life that remains steady becomes a testimony. When believers live with quiet integrity over time, people begin to notice. They may not agree with everything you believe, but they cannot ignore a faith that produces peace, resilience, and purpose.

This kind of witness does not require constant debate. It is carried in daily choices — how you treat others, how you speak, how you respond to pressure, how you endure hardship. A life shaped by truth sends a message even when words are few. It says that faith is not just an idea, but a foundation.

Many people who claim to reject Christianity are not actually rejecting Christ. They are rejecting shallow versions of Him. They have seen hypocrisy, fear, or compromise, and they have mistaken those things for faith. A believer who stands with humility and consistency offers a different picture. Over time, that picture can become more persuasive than any argument.

Standing for truth does not always lead to immediate change. But it always leaves a mark. Faithfulness plants seeds, even when we do not see them grow. A steady life rooted in Christ becomes a quiet invitation to others who are searching for something real.

When Standing Feels Lonely

Even when it is right, standing can feel isolating. There are moments when you look around and realize that fewer people are beside you than you expected. Conviction has a way of thinning the crowd. Not everyone is willing to pay the price of clarity, and when you do, it can feel as though you are walking alone.

But you are never as alone as you think.

Throughout history, God has always preserved a faithful remnant — people who quietly refused to bow, even when everyone else did. They did not always see one another, but they were never abandoned. The same is true now. There are believers all over the world who are choosing integrity over convenience, even when it costs them deeply.

Loneliness does not mean you are wrong. Often, it means you are early. Courage tends to move ahead of consensus. Those who stand first often feel the greatest weight of opposition, but they also make it easier for others to follow. When one person remains faithful, it gives others permission to do the same.

Standing is not about being surrounded by support. It is about being anchored in truth. And that anchor holds, even when the waves rise.

The Strength to Remain

Standing is not a single dramatic moment. It is a series of quiet, faithful decisions made over time. It is choosing to speak when it would be easier to stay silent. It is choosing integrity when compromise would bring comfort. It is choosing obedience when fear would suggest retreat. These choices may not make headlines, but they shape lives.

God does not call His people to be fearless. He calls them to be faithful. Courage is not the absence of fear; it is the decision to trust God more than the pressure around us. When believers learn to rest in that truth, standing becomes less about performance and more about perseverance.

The world may never fully understand those who refuse to bend. But it will feel the impact of their presence. A people who stand with clarity, humility, and love become a stabilizing force in a drifting culture. They remind others that truth is not a burden, but a foundation.

And when all is said and done, the measure of a life will not be how comfortable it was, but how faithful it was. Those who stand will not regret the cost. They will find that it was the very thing that gave their faith its depth and their witness its power.

PRAYER

Father,

Give us the courage to stand when standing is difficult. When fear whispers that silence is safer, remind us that obedience is better. Strengthen our hearts to choose truth over comfort, faithfulness over approval, and integrity over ease. Let us walk in Your truth with humility, grace, and unwavering conviction. In Jesus' name, Amen.

REFLECTION

1. Where in my life do I feel pressure to compromise or remain silent?

2. What fears most often keep me from standing for what I believe?

3. How might God be calling me to live with greater courage right now?

CHALLENGE

This week, identify one situation where you would normally stay quiet or avoid discomfort. Choose to respond with gentle honesty instead. Let it be a small but meaningful step toward becoming someone who stands with clarity and love, even when it is not easy.

8

THE BATTLE FOR THE NEXT GENERATION

Every generation inherits more than culture. It inherits a vision of reality. What children are taught to believe about truth, identity, and meaning will determine not only how they live, but what kind of world they create. This is why the struggle we are in is not primarily political or technological. It is generational. Whoever shapes the hearts and minds of the young shapes the future.

For the first time in modern history, many children are being raised in environments where faith is not just absent, but quietly undermined. They are taught that truth is fluid, that identity is self-created, and that moral boundaries are optional. God is rarely presented as real. He is presented as a concept — one belief among many, none of which are allowed to claim authority. Under this system, Christianity becomes a story rather than a foundation.

Parents often underestimate how powerful this influence is. A few hours a week in church cannot compete with dozens of hours of schooling, entertainment, and social media that carry a very different worldview. The messages are constant and consistent. Over time, they shape what feels normal. And what feels normal eventually feels true.

This is not because children are rebellious. It is because they are impressionable. They are absorbing the story the culture is telling them about who they are and what matters. If that story leaves God out, it will leave them unanchored. They may still believe in something spiritual, but they will not know why it matters.

The Church must recognize this moment for what it is. The next generation is not drifting away by accident. It is being discipled by a world that no longer believes in anything beyond itself. If that discipleship is left unchallenged, faith will not survive it.

The battle for the next generation is not about winning arguments.

It is about offering a better story.

The Story They Are Being Taught

Every child grows up inside a story. It tells them who they are, what the world is, and what they should live for. Today, that story is being written largely by screens, classrooms, and entertainment rather than by families or faith communities. It is a story that celebrates self-creation, emotional truth, and personal autonomy above everything else. In that story, the idea that God defines reality is not just ignored — it is quietly treated as dangerous.

This is why so many young people feel both empowered and deeply uncertain at the same time. They are told they can be anything, yet they have no stable answer to who they are. They are told to follow their hearts, yet their hearts are often confused. They are promised freedom, but not meaning. When God is removed from the center of the story, the self is forced to take His place — and the self is too fragile to carry that weight.

The result is not rebellion, but exhaustion. Many young people are tired of trying to invent themselves. They are anxious, overwhelmed, and unsure of what really matters. They sense that something is missing, even if they do not know how to name it. This is not a failure of youth. It is the predictable outcome of a culture that has handed them a story without transcendence.

The Church has an opportunity here. Not to condemn the next generation, but to understand it. Beneath the confusion is a hunger for something solid. Beneath the uncertainty is a longing for truth. If believers can offer a story rooted in God's reality — a story of purpose, belonging, and redemption — many will listen. The battle for the next generation will not be won by shouting, but by showing them that there is a better way to live.

Why Faith Feels Optional

One of the most subtle shifts in modern culture is how faith has been reclassified. It is no longer seen as something that describes reality. It is treated as a personal accessory — something you may choose if it helps you feel better, but not something that carries authority. For many young people, Christianity is not rejected; it is simply seen as irrelevant.

This is why walking away from church often feels so easy. If faith is only a private preference, then leaving it carries no real consequence. It is like changing a playlist or a hobby. But when faith is understood as a claim about what is true — about who God is and who we are — walking away becomes far more serious. The tragedy is that many have never been shown that version of Christianity.

Young people have not been taught to ask, "Is it true?"

They have been taught to ask, "Does it work for me?"

That question reshapes everything. Belief becomes something you keep only as long as it feels useful. When life becomes difficult or faith becomes inconvenient, it is easily discarded. But a belief that rests on usefulness will never survive suffering. Only a belief rooted in truth can do that.

The Church must recover its confidence in the reality of what it proclaims. The gospel is not a therapeutic tool. It is a declaration that God has acted in history and that His truth stands whether or not we find it convenient. When young people encounter a faith that is real rather than optional, many of them begin to listen in a different way.

The Role of Parents and Mentors

No institution has more influence on a child's faith than the people who walk with them every day. Parents, grandparents, teachers, and mentors shape not only what young people know, but what they trust. When faith is lived openly and honestly in the home, it becomes something real rather than theoretical. When it is hidden or avoided, it begins to feel irrelevant.

Many adults assume that children will simply absorb faith by being exposed to church. But belief is not contagious — it is cultivated. Young people watch how the adults around them handle fear, conflict, and suffering. They notice whether prayer is sincere or rushed, whether Scripture is treasured or ignored, whether God is treated as central or as an accessory. These daily signals speak louder than any sermon.

This is not about perfection. It is about authenticity. Children do not need flawless models of faith. They need honest ones. When they see adults wrestle with doubt, seek God in difficulty, and live with integrity, they learn that faith is not a performance — it is a relationship. That kind of example gives belief roots.

The battle for the next generation will not be won by programs alone. It will be won by people who live their faith in front of those they love. When young hearts see that following Christ brings meaning, stability, and hope, they are far more likely to listen when the world offers them something else.

Teaching Truth with Grace

One of the greatest challenges facing believers today is how to pass on truth in a culture that equates disagreement with harm. Many parents and leaders are afraid that if they speak clearly about what they believe, they will push young people away. But silence does not protect faith — it leaves it undefended. The goal is not to be harsh or controlling, but to be honest and loving at the same time.

Young people are not offended by conviction as much as they are offended by hypocrisy. They can sense when adults say one thing and live another. They can tell when beliefs are treated as optional rather than essential. What they need is not watered-down faith, but a faith that is strong enough to be trusted. Truth spoken with humility and consistency creates space for real dialogue.

This does not mean forcing beliefs on anyone. It means refusing to hide them. Children and students deserve to know what Christianity actually claims — about God, about humanity, and about the purpose of life. When truth is presented clearly and compassionately, it gives them something solid to engage with, whether they accept it immediately or not.

The battle for the next generation is not won by avoiding difficult topics. It is won by facing them with patience, wisdom, and love.

A Culture That Competes for Their Hearts

. . .

Young people today are not growing up in a neutral environment. They are surrounded by messages that constantly compete for their attention, loyalty, and identity. Social media, entertainment, and education all tell stories about what matters most, and those stories often contradict the values of faith. Without guidance, it is easy for these influences to become the primary teachers of the heart.

This does not mean the culture is entirely hostile. It means it is persuasive. It offers excitement, affirmation, and belonging. But it rarely offers meaning. When God is absent from the picture, success becomes hollow and freedom becomes fragile. Many young people sense this tension even if they cannot explain it. They are hungry for something that lasts.

Believers have a responsibility to engage this reality honestly. We cannot pretend the world our children are growing up in is the same one we knew. The pressures are different. The distractions are greater. The questions are more complex. But the human heart has not changed. It still longs for truth, purpose, and love.

When faith is presented as a living relationship with God rather than a set of rules, it becomes compelling in a world that is weary of shallow answers. The Church does not have to compete with culture by becoming like it. It must compete by offering something better.

Passing on a Living Faith

Faith cannot be preserved by silence. It is passed from one generation to the next through story, example, and relationship. When young people hear how God has worked in the lives of those they trust, belief becomes more than theory. It becomes something they can see and touch. Testimony gives faith a human face.

This is why intergenerational connection matters so deeply. Children need more than peers — they need guides. They need to see what it looks like to follow Christ through different seasons of life. They need to watch how faith sustains people in hardship, anchors them in uncertainty, and gives them hope beyond circumstances. These lived experiences teach more than any lesson ever could.

The Church is strongest when it functions as a family rather than a program. When relationships are deep and faith is shared openly, young people find a place where they belong. That sense of belonging is powerful. It gives them a reason to stay engaged even when questions and doubts arise.

The next generation is not lost. It is being formed. And those who choose to invest their time, love, and truth in them are shaping the future in ways they may never fully see.

A Hopeful Future

The battle for the next generation is not a story of inevitable decline. It is a story that is still being written. Even in a culture that often drifts from truth, young hearts remain open to meaning, purpose, and love. They are not closed to God — they are simply surrounded by noise. When that noise is quieted by authentic faith, many discover that they were searching for Him all along.

Believers should not approach this moment with fear. Fear leads to withdrawal, but faith leads to engagement. God has always worked through faithful people who were willing to love, teach, and stand in truth, even when the environment was difficult. The future of the Church does not depend on perfect conditions. It depends on faithful witnesses.

Every conversation matters. Every prayer matters. Every example of integrity leaves an imprint. When we invest in the next generation with patience and hope, we participate in something far larger than ourselves. We become part of God's work across time.

The story of faith has never ended with one generation. It continues through every heart that chooses to believe. And as long as that choice is made, hope remains strong.

PRAYER

Father,

We lift up the next generation to You. Protect their hearts from confusion and their minds from lies. Give them a hunger for what is true and a courage to seek You even when the world offers easier answers. Guide parents, mentors, and leaders to love well, speak clearly, and live faithfully. May Your truth take deep root in the hearts of those who will shape the future. In Jesus' name, Amen.

REFLECTION

1. What influences are shaping the beliefs of the young people in my life?

2. How am I personally modeling faith for the next generation?

3. Where might God be calling me to invest more intentionally in those who come after me?

CHALLENGE

Choose one young person—whether a child, student, or younger believer—and commit to encouraging them this week through prayer, conversation, or time spent together. Let your faith be something they can see, not just something they hear about.

9

WHEN TRUTH IS LABELED HATE

There was a time when disagreement could exist without destruction. People could hold opposing views and still share a table, a neighborhood, or a nation. That time is fading. In its place has come a new rule: to disagree is to be dangerous. To hold a moral conviction is to be accused of harm. And to speak a truth that challenges someone's identity is to be labeled hateful.

This shift has not happened by accident. It has been carefully shaped by a culture that has redefined love as affirmation and compassion as agreement. Under this new standard, truth is no longer something to be discovered — it is something to be negotiated. And any belief that refuses to bend becomes a threat.

For Christians, this creates a moral and spiritual crisis. The gospel is, by nature, exclusive. It makes claims about God, sin, salvation, and human purpose that cannot be reduced to personal preference. To follow Christ is to believe that some things are true and some things are not. But in a culture that demands emotional validation above all else, that kind of clarity is easily mistaken for cruelty.

The result is a growing pressure to remain silent on anything that might make someone uncomfortable. Biblical teachings about sexuality, identity, repentance, and holiness are especially targeted. They are not just disagreed with — they are portrayed as dangerous. Those who hold them are accused of being intolerant, unloving, or even violent in spirit.

This creates a powerful dilemma for believers. Speak, and risk being misunderstood. Remain silent, and risk betraying the truth. Many choose the second path, hoping to preserve peace. But peace built on silence is fragile. It requires the continual surrender of conviction.

The gospel has never fit neatly into any culture. It always confronts something. It always calls people to change. When that call is rebranded as hate, it becomes clear just how deeply the world has shifted.

How Language Was Rewritten

One of the most powerful tools used to silence truth is the manipulation of language. Words that once had clear meanings have been reshaped to serve a new moral framework. Love now means affirmation. Tolerance now means agreement. And hate has been expanded to include any belief that challenges personal identity or lifestyle. Under this system, disagreement itself becomes a moral offense.

This shift has made honest conversation nearly impossible. When every difference of belief is treated as a personal attack, people learn to protect themselves by avoiding difficult truths altogether. The goal is no longer to understand one another, but to avoid being accused. As a result, truth is not debated — it is policed.

Christians feel this pressure acutely. The teachings of Scripture are not vague or negotiable. They speak clearly about God's design for humanity, about sin, and about redemption. But when these teachings collide with modern cultural values, believers are told that their convictions are harmful. The accusation is not that Christians are wrong, but that they are dangerous.

This is a profound reversal. For centuries, faith was criticized as outdated or naive. Now it is framed as threatening. That framing makes it easier to justify exclusion, censorship, and hostility toward those who refuse to conform. It also creates fear. People begin to self-censor not because they doubt the truth, but because they dread the cost of being honest.

Yet when language is twisted, reality soon follows. If truth cannot be spoken, it cannot be known. And when truth disappears, confusion takes its place.

Why Conviction Feels So Threatening

Conviction has always unsettled cultures that define themselves by freedom. When people believe they can create their own meaning, any claim of objective truth feels like a restriction. It suggests that we are not the highest authority in our lives — and that idea is deeply uncomfortable in a world built on self-determination.

This is why Christian belief is not merely seen as different, but as oppressive. The gospel declares that God, not the individual, defines what is good and true. It insists that human desires must be brought under something higher. In a culture that elevates personal choice above everything else, this sounds like control rather than care.

But in reality, all freedom has boundaries. A world without moral limits does not produce happiness — it produces chaos. Yet when those boundaries come from God instead of from human opinion, they are resisted with unusual intensity. People do not want to be told that some choices lead to harm, even when the evidence is clear.

This is the deeper reason truth is labeled hate. It is not because Christians are cruel, but because conviction challenges the modern story of the self. It says we are created, not invented. It says our lives have purpose beyond our preferences. And that message strikes at the heart of a culture that has made autonomy its highest good.

Speaking Without Becoming Bitter

When truth is attacked, it is easy for believers to become defensive or angry. Being misunderstood hurts. Being labeled hateful feels unjust. Over time, that pain can harden the heart. But bitterness is not a sign of strength — it is a sign of woundedness. And wounded hearts do not speak with clarity.

Jesus never allowed opposition to turn Him cruel. He spoke hard truths, but He did so with compassion. He wept for those who rejected Him even as He confronted them. That balance is difficult, but it is essential. The goal is not to win arguments — it is to witness to truth in a way that reflects God's character.

Christians are called to speak honestly without becoming hostile. This means refusing to surrender conviction, but also refusing to surrender love. We do not have to mirror the anger of the culture to be heard. Quiet confidence is often more powerful than loud outrage.

When truth is spoken with humility, it cannot be dismissed as easily. Even when it is rejected, it leaves behind a sense that something real was offered. In a world that is quick to accuse and slow to listen, gentle courage stands out.

The Cost of Silence

Silence may feel like safety, but it carries a hidden cost. When believers stop speaking, they allow lies to grow unchecked. They allow confusion to harden into certainty. Over time, what was once questioned becomes accepted simply because no one challenged it. Silence does not preserve peace — it only postpones conflict while truth slowly erodes.

Many Christians choose quiet not because they no longer care, but because they are tired. They are weary of being misunderstood, of being judged, of being painted as villains. Yet when truth is abandoned, even temporarily, the consequences are real. Entire generations grow up without ever hearing a clear alternative to the dominant story of the culture.

The gospel was never meant to be hidden. It was meant to be shared, even when it is resisted. To love someone is not to let them remain in confusion, but to offer them something better. That offering will not always be welcomed, but it is always necessary.

Silence is comfortable in the moment, but costly in the long run. Faith that is never expressed eventually fades, not because it is false, but because it is never given room to live.

Truth and Love Are Not Enemies

One of the great deceptions of our time is the idea that truth and love are opposites. We are told that if something hurts someone's feelings, it cannot be loving, and if it challenges someone's choices, it must be hateful. But love that never tells the truth is not love at all. It is avoidance dressed up as kindness.

Real love seeks what is best, not just what is comfortable. A doctor who refuses to tell a patient the truth about their illness is not compassionate — he is negligent. In the same way, a faith that refuses to speak clearly about sin, redemption, and transformation is not merciful — it is silent.

Jesus never separated truth from love. He told people hard things because He cared deeply about them. He offered forgiveness, but He also called for repentance. He welcomed the broken, but He did not pretend brokenness was health. That balance is what makes the gospel powerful.

When Christians speak truth with humility and compassion, they reflect the heart of God. Even when their words are resisted, their love remains visible. And that visibility makes it harder to dismiss the truth as hate.

The Courage to Be Misunderstood

One of the greatest tests of faith is the willingness to be misunderstood. In a culture that values image and approval, few people are prepared for the discomfort of being seen as something they are not. Yet this has always been part of following Christ. Jesus Himself was called a blasphemer, a troublemaker, and a threat. Those who walked with Him were treated the same.

To stand for truth in this moment means accepting that your intentions may be misread. Your words may be twisted. Your character may be questioned. But faithfulness is not measured by how others perceive us — it is measured by how closely we align with what is true. The approval of God outweighs the opinions of the crowd.

This does not mean Christians should be careless or insensitive. It means they should not be controlled by fear of misunderstanding. When truth is at stake, the risk of being misjudged is often unavoidable. Courage is not the absence of that risk — it is the decision to speak anyway.

Those who are willing to be misunderstood for the sake of truth become anchors in uncertain times. They remind others that integrity still matters, even when it is inconvenient.

A Faith That Will Not Bend

. . .

There will always be pressure to soften the gospel so that it fits more comfortably into the culture of the moment. But a faith that is constantly reshaped by public opinion eventually loses its ability to speak with authority. Truth that bends to every wind is no longer truth — it is trend.

God does not call His people to be popular. He calls them to be faithful. That faithfulness may bring misunderstanding, resistance, or even hostility, but it also brings clarity. A Church that refuses to surrender its convictions becomes a lighthouse in a storm, guiding those who are lost toward something stable.

The world may call that stand hateful.

God calls it obedience.

And obedience, even when it is costly, always leads to life.

PRAYER

Father,

Give us hearts that love deeply and voices that speak truthfully. When the world confuses conviction with cruelty, help us remain faithful without becoming bitter. Teach us to reflect Your grace even when we are misunderstood. Let our words and lives point to what is real, even when it is resisted. In Jesus' name, Amen.

REFLECTION

1. Where have I felt pressure to stay silent about what I believe?

. . .

2. What truths do I find most difficult to speak in today's culture?

3. How can I grow in both courage and compassion at the same time?

CHALLENGE

This week, choose one moment to speak a difficult truth with kindness. It may be in a conversation, a message, or a simple statement of what you believe. Let it be gentle, but let it be honest. Faith grows stronger when it is lived out loud.

10

REBUILDING WHAT WAS LOST

Every collapse leaves behind more than rubble. It leaves behind a question. After the shaking, after the exposure, after the quiet failure of systems that once looked strong, something always remains. That something is not just what survived. It is what can be rebuilt. The future is not determined by what fell apart — it is determined by what rises in its place.

The modern Church has spent much of its energy trying to preserve what was. We have tried to hold on to old structures, old habits, and old assumptions about how faith fits into culture. But preservation is not the same as restoration. You cannot bring something back to life by pretending it never died. You bring it back by re-anchoring it to what made it alive in the first place.

What was lost was not influence.

What was lost was depth.

Faith was slowly hollowed out, not through open rebellion, but through accommodation. Belief became less about transformation and more about affirmation. Churches became less about discipleship and more about comfort. Over time, the power of the gospel was traded for the safety of social acceptance. And a faith that exists primarily to make people feel good eventually loses its ability to make people whole.

Rebuilding requires honesty. It requires admitting that some of what we called Christianity was actually just culture wearing religious language. We built programs instead of people. We emphasized attendance over obedience. We valued growth over holiness. These choices did not come from bad intentions, but they led to shallow foundations. And shallow foundations cannot hold when pressure comes.

The future of the Church will not be secured by better marketing or smoother messaging. It will be secured by a return to spiritual substance. We must recover what it means to actually follow Christ — not as a brand, not as an identity label, but as a daily surrender. That kind of faith does not fit neatly into cultural trends, but it endures when trends collapse.

This is not a call to retreat.

It is a call to rebuild.

Rebuilding begins with truth. It begins with Scripture taken seriously again. Not selectively, not symbolically, but as a living word that confronts, comforts, and corrects. A Church that does not know what it believes cannot lead anyone anywhere. When the Bible becomes optional, everything else becomes negotiable.

But when truth is restored to its rightful place, something powerful happens. Confusion gives way to clarity. Weakness gives way to strength. A people who know what they believe are no longer easily swayed by every new idea. They become rooted.

The Church does not need to be reinvented.

It needs to be remembered.

The earliest believers did not have influence, money, or political power. They had conviction, community, and the presence of God.

And that was enough to change the world. If we want to see renewal in our time, it will not come from copying the culture. It will come from standing apart from it with humility and courage.

Rebuilding what was lost will not be quick. It will not be comfortable. But it will be worth it. Because what rises from truth is always stronger than what falls from compromise.

Returning to First Principles

Rebuilding always begins with foundations. When something collapses, the question is not what we can salvage from the wreckage, but what we must lay again from the ground up. The Church does not need a new message. It needs a clear one. We must return to first principles — to the truths that gave the faith its power long before it had cultural support.

The first of these is the reality of God. Not a vague spirituality, not a distant force, but the living God who speaks, commands, loves, and judges. When God is reduced to an idea, faith becomes a hobby. When God is known as real, faith becomes a life. The early believers did not risk everything for a philosophy. They risked everything for a Person.

The second is the seriousness of sin. Modern culture treats sin as outdated language, but Scripture treats it as a condition of the heart that separates us from God and damages everything it touches. Without this truth, the gospel becomes meaningless. If nothing is wrong, nothing needs to be redeemed. But when sin is understood honestly, grace becomes precious again.

The third is the power of the cross. Jesus did not die to affirm us in our brokenness. He died to rescue us from it. The cross is not a symbol of comfort; it is a declaration of sacrifice. It tells us that God loves us enough to confront what is destroying us. When this truth is softened, the gospel loses its force.

The fourth is the call to repentance and obedience. Faith is not merely believing something is true — it is choosing to live as if it is. A gospel without transformation is not good news. The message of Christ is not simply that we are forgiven, but that we are being made new.

These are not optional beliefs. They are the bedrock of Christianity. If they are not rebuilt, nothing else will stand. Programs, politics, and popularity may create the appearance of strength, but only truth creates endurance.

A Church that returns to these first principles will not always be applauded. But it will be alive.

Reforming the Church from the Inside

True rebuilding never starts on the outside. It begins in the hearts of those who lead, teach, and live the faith. Structures can be adjusted, and programs can be redesigned, but without inner renewal, nothing changes. The greatest crisis facing the Church is not cultural hostility — it is spiritual shallowness. We have grown skilled at managing religion while neglecting transformation.

This is why repentance must come before revival. The Church cannot call the world to turn from sin while quietly tolerating it within its own walls. Integrity is not optional for a people who claim to carry truth. When leaders are compromised, when discipleship is neglected, and when holiness is treated as extreme, the witness of the Church is weakened from the inside out.

Rebuilding requires courageous self-examination. We must ask hard questions about what we have prioritized. Have we valued numbers over maturity? Have we chased relevance at the expense of faithfulness? Have we replaced prayer with strategy and Scripture with slogans? These are not comfortable questions, but they are necessary ones.

The Church was never meant to be a mirror of the culture. It was meant to be a contrast. When believers look no different from the world around them, something essential has been lost. But when faith is lived with sincerity and obedience, it becomes unmistakable.

Internal reform is not about becoming harsh or legalistic. It is about becoming honest. It is about returning to a life that is shaped by God's presence rather than by public opinion. That kind of reform does not draw attention to itself — but it changes everything.

Rebuilding Spiritual Habits

No lasting renewal is possible without a return to spiritual discipline. Faith grows where it is fed. It withers where it is neglected. Many of the weaknesses we see in the Church today are not the result of hostility from the world, but of neglect within. Prayer has been rushed. Scripture has been skimmed. Worship has been treated as optional. Over time, the inner life of believers has grown thin.

Rebuilding begins when these habits are restored. Prayer is not a ritual — it is communion. It is where believers draw strength, wisdom, and perspective. When prayer is neglected, faith becomes anxious and reactive. When prayer is practiced, faith becomes steady.

Scripture is not just a source of inspiration. It is the foundation of truth. A Church that does not know the Word cannot stand against confusion. When the Bible is studied deeply and applied honestly, it shapes how people think, live, and love. Without it, faith drifts.

Worship, too, is more than music. It is the alignment of the heart with God's reality. It reminds believers who they are and who God is. In a culture that constantly pulls attention outward, worship brings it back to what matters most.

These disciplines may not look dramatic, but they are powerful. They build resilience. They anchor identity. They prepare believers to stand when pressure comes. Rebuilding the Church will not begin with crowds. It will begin with people who are rooted.

Reclaiming Community

The Church was never meant to be a crowd. It was meant to be a body. Believers were designed to grow together, support one another, and carry one another through seasons of weakness and doubt. Yet in many places, community has been replaced by convenience. People attend services but remain unknown. They listen to sermons but never share their struggles. The result is isolation inside a room full of people.

Rebuilding what was lost requires restoring real connection. Discipleship does not happen in rows — it happens in relationships. Faith is strengthened when people pray together, confess together, and walk together. When believers know they are not alone, they are more willing to take risks, speak truth, and stand firm.

This kind of community is not always comfortable. It requires vulnerability. It requires accountability. It requires time. But it also produces depth. A Church that is built on genuine relationships becomes a refuge in a fractured world. It offers belonging without compromise and support without deception.

In a culture where loneliness is rising, authentic Christian community is one of the most powerful witnesses we have. It shows that faith is not just about beliefs, but about people. Rebuilding the Church means creating spaces where people are not just welcomed, but known.

Raising Leaders of Conviction

. . .

Every lasting movement rises or falls on the quality of its leaders. The Church does not need more celebrities or strategists — it needs shepherds with backbone. Leaders who know what they believe, why they believe it, and who are willing to stand for it when the cost is high. Rebuilding what was lost requires a new generation of leadership rooted in conviction rather than popularity.

Too many have been trained to manage institutions instead of guard truth. They have learned how to grow platforms but not how to grow souls. When leadership is driven by image, the message is softened. When leadership is driven by fear, truth is withheld. But when leadership is driven by obedience, the Church becomes strong.

Raising leaders of conviction begins with discipleship. It means training people not only in what Scripture says, but in how to live it. It means forming character before competence. It means valuing faithfulness more than success. Leaders who have been shaped by prayer, suffering, and humility are not easily swayed by cultural pressure.

The future of the Church depends on men and women who are willing to carry the weight of truth without dropping it. These leaders will not always be popular. But they will be trusted. And trust is far more powerful than applause.

Building for the Long Term

Rebuilding is not about quick wins. It is about creating something that will still stand when trends change and attention moves on. The Church has too often been tempted to chase immediate results — bigger crowds, louder voices, faster growth. But strength is not measured by speed. It is measured by stability.

What lasts is built slowly, through faithfulness repeated over time. It is built through prayer that does not stop when answers are delayed.

It is built through teaching that does not change when it becomes unpopular. It is built through relationships that endure when conflict arises. These are the quiet bricks that form a strong foundation.

The next season of the Church will belong to those who are willing to invest deeply rather than expand quickly. Shallow growth collapses under pressure. Deep roots hold firm. A people grounded in truth, connected in community, and led by conviction will not be easily shaken.

God is not in a hurry. He is building something eternal. When we align ourselves with that work, we learn to value faithfulness over flash and endurance over excitement. That shift changes everything.

What Will Rise

Every collapse creates space. When old structures fall, new ones can be built. The question is not whether something will rise — it is what will rise. If the Church does not rebuild on truth, something else will fill the void. The future will be shaped either by conviction or by confusion.

God has not abandoned His people. He is purifying them. He is stripping away what was shallow so that what is real can remain. This moment is not a death sentence — it is a refining fire. What comes out of it can be stronger, truer, and more faithful than what went in.

The Church that rises will not look like the one that fell. It will be less concerned with image and more devoted to obedience. It will be less focused on influence and more focused on integrity. It will be smaller in some places, but deeper everywhere. It will be led by people who fear God more than they fear losing approval.

This is not a season to despair.

It is a season to build.

Those who choose to stand now will become the foundation for what comes next. Their faithfulness will shape the future long after this cultural moment has passed. What rises from truth will always outlast what falls from compromise.

PRAYER

Father,

We ask You to rebuild what has been weakened in us and in Your Church. Restore depth where there has been drift, conviction where there has been compromise, and faithfulness where there has been fear. Teach us to build on Your truth, not on comfort or approval. Let what rises from this season be stronger, purer, and more alive than what came before. In Jesus' name, Amen.

REFLECTION

1. What areas of my faith have become shallow or neglected?

2. Where might God be calling me to return to deeper spiritual habits?

3. How can I contribute to rebuilding the Church where I am?

CHALLENGE

Choose one spiritual habit that has weakened—prayer, Scripture, or fellowship—and commit to restoring it this week. Let it be a deliberate step toward becoming someone who is rooted, resilient, and ready to build what comes next.

11

THE RISE OF A REMNANT

Every great spiritual renewal in history has begun the same way — not with the majority, but with a faithful few. When culture drifts and institutions weaken, God does not wait for everyone to come back. He calls a remnant. A small, determined group of people who refuse to surrender truth, even when it is unpopular. These are the ones through whom lasting change is born.

A remnant is not defined by size. It is defined by commitment. They are people who have decided that obedience matters more than approval, and that faith is worth the cost. They do not wait for conditions to be ideal. They stand when standing is lonely. They pray when praying feels pointless. They remain faithful when faith seems foolish.

In times of cultural collapse, most people look for safety. A remnant looks for faithfulness. They understand that comfort is temporary, but truth is eternal. Their lives are not driven by trends or fear, but by conviction. That conviction becomes a light in the darkness, drawing others who are hungry for something real.

The Bible is filled with stories of such people. Noah stood alone when the world was corrupt. Elijah believed when everyone else bowed to false gods. The early Church grew not because it was powerful, but because it was faithful. God has always worked through those who are willing to be different.

We are living in another such moment. As confusion increases and compromise becomes normal, those who remain anchored in truth will begin to stand out. They will not always be celebrated. But they will be noticed. And in that noticing, the seeds of renewal are planted.

The rise of a remnant is not a retreat from the world.

It is the beginning of its restoration.

How a Remnant Is Formed

A remnant is not created through enthusiasm. It is formed through testing. God does not gather His most faithful people by offering them ease; He refines them through pressure. Those who remain when it becomes difficult are the ones who are truly committed. Comfort reveals preferences. Difficulty reveals conviction.

This is why seasons of cultural hostility toward faith are not just threats — they are filters. When standing for truth costs nothing, many will claim it. But when standing begins to require sacrifice, only those who truly believe will stay. This is not something to fear. It is something to understand. God has always used moments of separation to strengthen His people.

The remnant is shaped in places most people try to avoid: in loneliness, in criticism, in the tension of being misunderstood. When believers are pushed to the margins, they are forced to decide what really matters. Will they cling to acceptance, or will they cling to truth? That decision forms the spine of their faith.

Over time, this produces a people who are not easily shaken. They have faced rejection and survived. They have been questioned and held their ground. Their faith is no longer theoretical. It has been proven. And proven faith carries authority.

This is why cultural pressure often precedes spiritual renewal. When the cost of discipleship rises, shallow belief falls away. What remains is a smaller but stronger Church. A Church that knows what it believes and why it believes it. A Church that is no longer confused about its identity.

The remnant does not separate itself out of arrogance. It is separated by reality. Truth creates distinction. Light creates contrast. A people who live by God's standards will naturally stand apart in a world that lives by its own.

And that distinction is powerful.

In a culture saturated with confusion, clarity becomes magnetic. People who are tired of drifting begin to notice those who are anchored. They are drawn not by perfection, but by stability. A remnant that walks with integrity becomes a signpost pointing toward something solid.

This is how movements begin. Not with crowds, but with consistency. Not with noise, but with depth. A handful of faithful people can do more than a thousand who are merely enthusiastic.

God is not looking for a majority.

He is looking for a people who will not move.

And when He finds them, He builds through them.

Why God Works Through the Few

History rarely changes because of majorities. It changes because of minorities who refuse to yield. God has always moved this way, not because He lacks power, but because He is forming people, not just producing outcomes. A remnant carries more spiritual weight than a crowd because it has been shaped by faithfulness rather than convenience.

The few who stand when it is difficult become the moral backbone of their time. They do not drift with opinion. They do not shift with trends. They live from a deeper place — one that is anchored in truth rather than in acceptance. When a culture is confused, it needs people who are clear. When it is afraid, it needs people who are steady. That steadiness is not born in comfort. It is forged in conviction.

God allows His people to experience opposition because it reveals what is real. When belief is tested, it either deepens or disappears. A remnant is made up of those whose faith deepens. They no longer believe simply because they were raised that way. They believe because they have chosen to, again and again, even when it was costly. Their faith is no longer borrowed — it is owned.

This kind of faith cannot be manufactured. It is built through obedience in small, unseen moments. It grows when people choose integrity over ease, prayer over distraction, and truth over popularity. Over time, those choices compound. What emerges is a people who carry spiritual authority, not because they seek it, but because they have earned it through faithfulness.

The world is starving for that kind of authenticity. People are weary of shallow performances and hollow slogans. They are searching for something that feels real. A remnant offers that reality. It does not have to announce itself. It simply lives in a way that cannot be ignored. There is a quiet power in a life that refuses to bend.

God does not need large numbers to change a nation. He needs hearts that are wholly His. When those hearts come together, something unstoppable begins to form. The few who are willing to stand become the foundation for the many who will one day follow.

The rise of a remnant is never the end of the story.

It is the beginning of renewal.

What the Remnant Is Called to Become

A remnant is not merely a group that survives. It is a people who are being shaped for responsibility. God does not preserve a faithful few so that they can remain hidden; He prepares them so that they can carry what others have dropped. In every season of decline, God is quietly building leaders, intercessors, teachers, and servants who will one day be entrusted with something far larger than themselves.

The remnant is called to maturity. This means growing beyond shallow belief into disciplined, resilient faith. It means learning to pray when emotions are absent, to obey when circumstances are difficult, and to trust when outcomes are uncertain. These are not glamorous traits, but they are essential. They create a people who are not easily discouraged or distracted.

In a culture that has grown addicted to affirmation, the remnant must learn to live without it. Their identity cannot be rooted in applause or approval. It must be rooted in God. When this shift happens, fear loses its power. Criticism no longer controls. The remnant becomes free — not because life becomes easier, but because their allegiance becomes clearer.

God is forming a people who can withstand misunderstanding without becoming bitter, who can face opposition without becoming hostile, and who can endure isolation without becoming proud. This kind of character is rare because it requires humility as much as courage. It is far easier to shout than to remain steady. It is far easier to react than to remain faithful.

The remnant is not called to withdraw from the world, but to engage it from a different place. They are meant to carry truth with gentleness, conviction with compassion, and clarity with grace. This combination is powerful because it cannot be easily dismissed. It reflects the heart of Christ Himself.

What God is building through the remnant is not a counterculture of anger, but a culture of holiness. Not a movement of outrage, but a movement of integrity. The world does not need more people who are merely loud. It needs people who are deep.

The remnant will not be recognized by how much noise it makes, but by how much weight it carries. And that weight will come from lives that have been shaped by truth, sacrifice, and love.

How a Remnant Becomes a Movement

A remnant does not exist for the purpose of survival. It exists for the purpose of restoration. God never preserves a faithful few so that they can remain hidden. He preserves them so that they can become the foundation for what comes next. What begins as obedience in isolation eventually becomes influence in community. That is how movements are born.

At first, a remnant looks insignificant. It has no platform, no recognition, no visible power. But what it does have is something far more important: shared conviction. These are people who have already paid the price of standing. They have already been misunderstood, criticized, or ignored. They have already chosen faithfulness over comfort. That common experience creates a powerful bond. When such people find one another, something shifts. They realize they are not alone. Their courage multiplies.

This is how isolated believers become connected leaders. They stop thinking of themselves as exceptions and begin to see themselves as part of something God is doing. Conversations deepen. Prayer intensifies. Vision begins to form. The remnant becomes aware that it was not preserved by accident. It was preserved for a purpose.

Every true movement begins when people stop waiting for permission and start living with intention. They do not wait for institutions to validate them. They do not wait for culture to approve of them. They act because truth demands action. They begin creating spaces for discipleship, for honest conversation, for courageous faith. Small gatherings become communities. Communities become networks. Networks become movements.

What drives this growth is not ambition. It is alignment. When people are aligned around truth, clarity, and purpose, they move in the same direction even without centralized control. The remnant becomes a decentralized force — not organized by hierarchy, but unified by conviction. That kind of unity is resilient. It does not collapse when leaders fall or circumstances change. It is carried in the hearts of the people themselves.

A remnant becomes a movement when it stops seeing itself as reacting to the world and starts seeing itself as responsible for it. God does not call His people merely to resist darkness, but to bring light. This requires vision. It requires imagining what faithfulness could look like in families, churches, schools, and communities. It requires building something better, not just criticizing what is broken.

This is the moment when Faith Vanguard becomes more than a warning. It becomes a calling. It calls people out of quiet frustration and into visible, purposeful faith. It challenges believers to stop waiting for revival and to start living like they are part of it. When conviction is paired with action, faith becomes contagious.

The world is not changed by large numbers of passive people.

It is changed by small numbers of active ones.

A faithful remnant that knows who it is and what it stands for becomes unstoppable. Not because it seeks power, but because it carries truth. And truth, when it is lived boldly and shared freely, always finds a way to grow.

. . .

What the Remnant Must Build

A remnant that only resists the culture will eventually be exhausted by it. To survive, and more importantly to transform the world, it must begin to build. Resistance slows decay. Construction creates a future. God does not gather His faithful people merely to survive collapse; He gathers them to lay new foundations.

The remnant must build spiritual infrastructure. Not institutions obsessed with image, but systems designed to produce disciples. The Church drifted not because it lacked activity, but because it lacked formation. People were attending services without being shaped by them. They were listening without being discipled. The remnant must reverse that pattern.

What is needed now are environments where truth is not diluted and faith is not optional. Places where Scripture is taught deeply, where prayer is practiced consistently, and where obedience is expected lovingly. These do not have to be large. They must be strong. God has always done His most powerful work through small groups of deeply committed people.

The remnant must also build relationships that are thick enough to carry weight. Shallow connections collapse under pressure. But real community — people who know one another, pray for one another, and walk together through difficulty — creates resilience. This is where courage grows. This is where accountability lives. This is where faith becomes sustainable.

A movement cannot be built on crowds. It must be built on people. People who are known. People who are trained. People who are trusted. This is how leadership is born. Not from talent alone, but from character tested over time. The remnant must become a training ground for leaders who are unafraid of truth and unmoved by pressure.

Faith Vanguard is not meant to be a brand. It is meant to be a backbone. A structure of belief and community that allows people to stand when the culture shifts. When believers know they are not alone, they become braver. When they know they are supported, they become stronger. When they know they are part of something real, they become dangerous to the forces of confusion.

What the remnant builds now will shape the future of the Church. These foundations will determine whether faith can endure the storms ahead. God is calling His people not just to speak, but to build — to create something that can carry truth forward long after this moment has passed.

This is not about retreat.

This is about legacy.

Taking Responsibility for the Future

Every generation inherits more than land, laws, or technology. It inherits a moral and spiritual atmosphere shaped by the courage or compromise of those who came before. We are living inside a world that was built by the decisions of yesterday, and the world that will exist tomorrow is being shaped right now by what we choose to stand for—or what we choose to ignore. The remnant must understand this clearly: history does not move forward by accident. It moves forward on the strength or weakness of conviction.

What is being lost in our time is not simply tradition. It is truth that has been left undefended. When a culture abandons moral clarity, it does not become more free. It becomes more confused. When a generation grows up without firm foundations, it does not become more open-minded. It becomes more anxious. The cost of compromise is always paid by those who did not choose it. Children inherit the consequences of the faith their parents failed to live.

This is why the remnant cannot afford to be passive. Faith that is not intentionally passed on is eventually forgotten. In a world saturated with messages that compete for the hearts of the young, silence is not neutral—it is surrender. If believers do not actively shape the spiritual environment of their families and communities, something else will. And that something else will not lead to truth, stability, or life.

The remnant is being called to think beyond the moment. We are not just called to survive this cultural storm. We are called to build something strong enough to outlast it. That means raising children who know why they believe, not just what they believe. It means forming young adults who can stand in truth without becoming cruel and love without becoming confused. It means creating communities where faith is not a weekend habit, but a way of life.

This work cannot be outsourced. No institution, no program, no church building can replace the daily witness of faithful adults. Children learn what matters by watching how we handle pressure, conflict, and sacrifice. They notice whether prayer is real or performative. They notice whether Scripture shapes decisions or sits quietly on a shelf. They notice whether God is central or convenient.

If the remnant is to become a movement, it must become a culture of intentional discipleship. Not just teaching, but modeling. Not just instruction, but imitation. Faith must be lived in front of the next generation with consistency, humility, and courage. When young people see adults who are willing to lose comfort for the sake of truth, they begin to understand that faith is not just something you say—it is something you are.

This kind of generational formation is slow, but it is powerful. It does not produce instant results, but it produces lasting ones. A child who grows up in an environment where faith is respected, practiced, and protected carries something into adulthood that no ideology can easily erase. A young person who has seen God work in real lives does not easily dismiss Him as a myth.

The remnant must also be willing to reclaim its role as a moral anchor in the wider culture. We cannot allow the next generation to grow up believing that truth is cruel and conviction is dangerous. We must show them that truth, when carried with love, is life-giving. We must show them that clarity is not oppression, but protection. And we must show them that God's ways are not outdated—they are enduring.

God did not preserve His faithful people through seasons of confusion so that they could quietly fade away. He preserved them so that they could carry light into a dark future. The remnant is not an echo of the past. It is the seed of what is coming.

What we build now will determine what survives later.

The faith we fight for today will become the foundation that others stand on tomorrow.

And the courage we choose in this moment will become the inheritance of generations we may never meet.

The Moment We Were Born For

Every generation is given a moment that defines it. A point in history where neutrality is no longer possible and where the future depends on the courage of the present. This is that moment. The confusion of the age, the collapse of moral clarity, and the hunger for something real are not coincidences — they are conditions ripe for renewal.

God does not place His people in difficult times by accident. He places them there on purpose. When truth is rare, it becomes powerful. When faith is costly, it becomes meaningful. The remnant that has been refined through pressure is now being positioned for impact. What was forged in obscurity is being prepared for influence.

This is not about returning to a golden age that no longer exists. It is about building something better than what was lost. A Church that is not afraid to be different. A faith that does not need cultural approval to be confident. A people who know who they are because they know whose they are.

Faith Vanguard is not simply a name. It is a calling. It represents a generation of believers who refuse to retreat, refuse to compromise, and refuse to be silent. They are not driven by anger. They are driven by love for what is true. They understand that standing in truth is the most loving thing they can do for a world that has lost its way.

The remnant does not wait for permission.

It does not ask for applause.

It moves because it must.

This is the moment we were born for.

And what we do now will echo far beyond our own lives.

PRAYER

Father,

Thank You for calling us to this moment. Give us hearts that are faithful when it would be easier to retreat and courage that remains when it would be safer to blend in. Shape us into people who carry Your truth with humility, strength, and love. Use us to build something that will bless generations we may never see. In Jesus' name, Amen.

REFLECTION

1. Where has God been asking me to stand more firmly in truth?

. . .

2. What fears have kept me from fully embracing that calling?

3. How might my faith today shape the future of those who come after me?

CHALLENGE

Choose one way you can invest in the future this week—by mentoring someone, deepening a relationship, or strengthening a spiritual habit. Let your faith be something that builds, not just something that believes.

12

THE COST OF CONVICTION

Conviction is easy to admire and hard to live. Everyone loves the idea of standing for something until standing actually costs them something. In every generation, people praise courage in the past while avoiding it in the present. We honor those who resisted tyranny, spoke truth, or refused to bow—but when that same kind of courage is required now, it suddenly feels uncomfortable, divisive, or extreme. Yet history makes one thing painfully clear: truth has always required a price.

The Western church has grown deeply uncomfortable with that price. We have learned to speak about faith in ways that are safe, marketable, and socially acceptable. We are willing to affirm spiritual values, but not moral authority. We celebrate love, but avoid truth. We sing about Jesus, but hesitate to follow Him when His teachings clash with culture. This has produced a generation of Christians who believe deeply in their hearts but live cautiously in public, afraid that conviction might lead to rejection.

Jesus never offered that kind of faith. He never promised safety, approval, or comfort. He promised life—but only through surrender. He warned that those who follow Him would be misunderstood, opposed, and sometimes even hated. Not because they were cruel, but because truth always disrupts systems built on lies. Light exposes what darkness depends on. That is why conviction has always been threatening to the world.

The problem today is not that Christians lack belief. It is that many lack the willingness to let that belief shape their choices when it becomes inconvenient. We pray boldly in private, but soften our words in public. We agree with Scripture, but hesitate to speak it. We know what is right, but we fear the consequences of saying so. Over time, this creates a faith that is sincere but quiet, passionate but hidden, genuine but restrained.

That restraint comes at a cost. When conviction is muted, confusion grows. When truth is avoided, lies gain ground. When believers retreat, culture advances unchecked. The church does not lose influence all at once—it loses it slowly, one compromise at a time. Each moment we choose comfort over clarity, the lines between truth and opinion blur just a little more.

Conviction is not about being loud or angry. It is about being anchored. It is about knowing what you believe so deeply that you are willing to live differently because of it. It is the quiet strength to say no when everyone else says yes, to stand firm when pressure mounts, and to remain faithful when the cost rises. That kind of conviction is rare, but it is also powerful. It shapes families, churches, and even nations.

The world does not need more Christians who are simply kind. It needs Christians who are courageous. Kindness without conviction becomes sentimentality. Compassion without truth becomes confusion. Love without boundaries becomes meaningless. True faith holds all of these together—grace and truth, humility and boldness, gentleness and strength.

Every generation is tested. Not by how loudly it claims belief, but by how faithfully it lives it. The question facing the modern church is not whether it still believes in God. The question is whether it is still willing to stand for Him when that stand is no longer popular.

Conviction always reveals what matters most. And in this moment of cultural pressure, what the church chooses to do next will tell the world exactly who it truly serves.

The Cost of Conviction

If conviction costs nothing, it means it is worth nothing. Throughout history, the truth has never been the popular path, and those who chose to walk it have always been required to sacrifice something—status, comfort, relationships, reputation, or safety. The reason conviction carries a price is because it collides directly with human pride, cultural momentum, and spiritual resistance. To live by conviction is to choose alignment with God over alignment with the world.

Yet modern Christianity has been trained to avoid that collision. Many believers have been taught—subtly or explicitly—that faith should fit neatly inside existing social structures rather than challenge them. We are encouraged to be "winsome," agreeable, and non-confrontational, even when those virtues become excuses for silence. In trying to remain palatable, we have lost our edge. And in losing our edge, we have lost our voice.

The culture around us has not become hostile to Christianity because Christians have become too harsh. It has become hostile because Christianity still carries moral weight. Even watered-down faith contains an authority that unsettles a world built on self-definition. Truth has gravity. It pulls against everything that resists it. That is why conviction feels heavy—because it carries the weight of eternity.

When Christians avoid conviction, it is rarely because they do not believe. It is because belief has not yet outweighed fear. Fear of being labeled. Fear of being misunderstood. Fear of losing influence, relationships, or opportunities. But Scripture never treats fear as neutral.

Fear is always a master, and it always demands obedience. When fear governs faith, compromise follows.

This is how the church becomes quiet while the world grows loud. Not because truth has vanished, but because courage has. Not because the gospel has lost power, but because believers have stopped wielding it. And when conviction fades, the church does not merely lose relevance—it loses its calling.

Jesus never invited people to a life of convenience. He invited them to a cross. That invitation still stands. A cross is not a symbol of comfort. It is a symbol of surrender. It means laying down control, safety, and self-protection in exchange for obedience. That kind of faith cannot be managed. It cannot be safely contained within social approval. It changes everything it touches.

Many Christians today are trying to follow Jesus without carrying His weight. They want the hope of heaven without the tension of discipleship. They want the benefits of faith without the burden of faithfulness. But conviction does not work that way. It demands coherence between what you believe and how you live. It requires alignment between confession and conduct.

When conviction is strong, it reshapes priorities. You stop measuring success by applause and start measuring it by obedience. You stop asking what will be easiest and start asking what will be right. You stop negotiating with truth and begin submitting to it. That is when faith becomes more than sentiment—it becomes substance.

This kind of conviction does not produce arrogance. It produces clarity. It does not create hostility; it creates direction. It does not push people away; it gives them something real to encounter. A church that stands firmly may be resisted, but it will never be ignored. People hunger for truth, even when they argue with it.

The tragedy of our time is not that the world rejects God. It is that the church has grown unsure of Him. When conviction wavers, the church begins to mirror the culture instead of confronting it. And when that happens, the very thing meant to bring light becomes indistinguishable from the darkness.

Conviction is not a weapon—it is a witness. It tells the world that something greater than comfort exists. Something greater than popularity. Something greater than fear. And when Christians live with that kind of clarity, even opposition becomes a platform.

The question is no longer whether conviction is costly. The question is whether the church is still willing to pay.

The Cost of Conviction

Conviction is not merely what you believe when it is safe to believe it. It is what you cling to when believing becomes dangerous. It is easy to affirm truth when it is socially rewarded. It is far harder when truth isolates you, when it draws a line between you and people you care about, when it forces you to choose between belonging and obedience. That is where real faith is revealed—not in comfort, but in conflict.

Every generation of believers faces a moment when neutrality is no longer an option. A moment when silence becomes a form of betrayal. We are living in one of those moments now. The cultural ground beneath us has shifted so rapidly that what was once assumed has become contested, and what was once protected has become mocked. In such a climate, conviction is no longer invisible. It is visible. And anything visible becomes vulnerable.

This is why so many retreat. It is not that they no longer know what is true. It is that they no longer know if they are willing to be known for it. In a world that punishes disagreement, conviction becomes a liability. But Scripture has always framed conviction as a calling. "Choose this day whom you will serve," was never meant to be a poetic line—it was a demand for decision.

What makes conviction costly is not simply external pressure. It is the internal struggle between who we want to be and who God is calling us to become. Faith forces us to confront our desire for acceptance. It exposes the places where we have traded obedience for approval. And when those two collide, something must give.

Modern culture rewards flexibility. It celebrates those who can shift, adapt, and redefine themselves endlessly. Conviction, by contrast, insists that some things are fixed. That truth is not negotiable. That identity is not self-created. That moral reality exists beyond opinion. This is why conviction feels so disruptive—it challenges the illusion of total autonomy.

Yet without conviction, faith becomes little more than a lifestyle accessory. Something we wear when it fits and remove when it becomes uncomfortable. But true faith does not function like fashion. It is not meant to match the season. It is meant to anchor the soul.

When believers lose conviction, they do not become more compassionate. They become more confused. Without a clear moral center, love becomes sentimentality. Without truth, grace becomes permission. And without courage, mercy becomes silence. The church may appear gentle, but it has lost its power.

Jesus never softened the truth to make it easier to receive. He spoke with clarity because clarity is an act of love. A doctor who hides a diagnosis does not show compassion—he shows cowardice. In the same way, a church that refuses to speak truth is not protecting people; it is abandoning them.

Conviction protects the soul from drift. It keeps us from being slowly pulled away by cultural currents that promise freedom but deliver emptiness. It guards the heart against compromise that begins small and ends in surrender. Without conviction, faith erodes not in one dramatic collapse but in a thousand quiet concessions.

This is why conviction must be formed before it is tested. When pressure comes, you do not rise to the occasion—you fall to the level of your preparation. If your faith is shallow, it will collapse under weight. If it is rooted, it will hold. Conviction grows in private long before it is displayed in public.

We must understand what is at stake. This is not merely about winning arguments or preserving traditions. It is about whether truth will still have a voice in a generation being trained to distrust it. It is about whether the church will stand as a pillar or dissolve into an echo.

The cost of conviction is real. But the cost of losing it is far greater.

What We Are Really Afraid Of

Beneath every compromise lies a fear that few people are willing to name. We do not abandon conviction because we suddenly stop believing what is true. We abandon it because we become afraid of what truth will cost us. That fear may take many forms—rejection, ridicule, career risk, relational loss, or public shame—but it always traces back to the same root: the fear of losing our place in the world.

Belonging is one of the deepest human needs. We are wired to be part of something, to be known, to be accepted. That desire is not wrong—it was placed in us by God. But when belonging becomes more important than obedience, it begins to rule us. We start making small adjustments, small concessions, small edits to what we say and how we live. None of them feel dramatic at first. They feel reasonable. They feel safe. And that is precisely what makes them dangerous.

The culture we live in has become extremely skilled at weaponizing social fear. It does not need to arrest or imprison people to control them. It simply needs to isolate them. Public shaming, online outrage, and professional consequences have become powerful tools of discipline. People learn very quickly what happens when they say the wrong thing. And once they have seen someone else be punished, they begin to self-censor.

This is how a society changes without laws ever being passed.

People simply become afraid to speak.

Christians are not immune to this pressure. Many know what Scripture teaches, but they hesitate to say it out loud. They fear being labeled hateful, ignorant, or extreme. They fear being misunderstood by coworkers, neighbors, or even family members. And so they choose silence—not because they agree with the culture, but because they do not want to be pushed out of it.

But silence has consequences. When truth is not spoken, it does not disappear—it is replaced. Lies rush into the empty space. Confusion fills the vacuum. Over time, what was once unthinkable becomes normalized simply because no one is willing to challenge it. This is how entire moral frameworks shift without most people ever consciously choosing them.

The tragedy is that many believers think they are protecting peace. They think that staying quiet will preserve relationships. They think that avoiding conflict will keep doors open. But relationships built on suppressed truth are fragile. They require constant self-betrayal to maintain. Eventually, the cost of staying silent becomes greater than the cost of speaking.

What we are really afraid of is being alone. We fear losing our tribe, our reputation, our place at the table. But faith has always required a willingness to stand even when standing feels lonely. Noah stood alone. Elijah stood alone. The early Christians stood alone. They did not do so because they enjoyed conflict, but because they loved truth more than comfort.

Jesus Himself warned His followers that allegiance to Him would divide relationships. Not because He wanted division, but because truth reveals priorities. When faith collides with fear, one will always win. And what wins determines who we become.

Many Christians today feel an internal fracture. They believe deeply, but live cautiously. They pray boldly, but speak softly. They feel conviction in their hearts, but hesitation in their voices. That inner division creates exhaustion. We were never meant to live at odds with our own beliefs. Integrity brings peace. Compromise brings tension.

Conviction is not what makes us harsh. Fear is. When people are afraid, they become reactive, defensive, and brittle. When people are anchored in truth, they become calm, steady, and clear. Real conviction does not need to shout. It does not need to insult. It simply stands.

The world does not actually hate conviction. It hates being confronted by it. Truth exposes what is false. Light reveals what has been hidden. That is uncomfortable. But discomfort is often the doorway to change. A faith that refuses to cause discomfort has lost its power to heal.

The cost of conviction is real.

But the cost of fear is far greater.

Fear produces a church that is quiet, unsure, and internally divided. Conviction produces a church that is steady, courageous, and whole. One retreats. The other advances. One blends in. The other becomes a beacon.

Every believer must decide which price they are willing to pay.

The price of standing...

or the price of shrinking.

What Conviction Actually Costs

The cost of conviction is rarely paid all at once. It is paid slowly, quietly, and repeatedly. It is paid in conversations where you choose honesty instead of harmony. It is paid in moments when you could stay silent but choose to speak. It is paid when you sense that telling the truth will make things awkward, complicated, or uncomfortable

—and you do it anyway. This is how conviction becomes real. Not through grand gestures, but through a thousand small acts of faithfulness.

Most people imagine the cost of conviction as something dramatic: persecution, arrest, or public confrontation. But in modern life, it is far more subtle and therefore far more dangerous. The cost is often relational. It is the raised eyebrow from a friend. The tension at a family gathering. The quiet distancing from coworkers. The shift in tone when people realize you will not simply go along with whatever is popular. These small social penalties add up. Over time, they wear down resolve. They tempt believers to soften, to edit, to slowly become less visible.

This is how faith is hollowed out. Not by outright denial, but by gradual retreat.

People begin to choose their words carefully. They avoid certain topics. They change the way they phrase their beliefs. Eventually, they begin to change what they believe they are allowed to believe. Conviction becomes something private, hidden, disconnected from daily life. Faith becomes something that exists inside the heart but not in the world. And a faith that does not shape the world eventually stops shaping the heart.

There is a spiritual danger in trying to be acceptable to everyone. The desire to be liked is natural, but when it becomes dominant, it turns into a form of worship. Approval becomes the god we serve. We begin to ask, "How will this make me look?" instead of, "Is this true?" That shift happens quietly, but it changes everything. When approval becomes the highest good, truth becomes expendable.

Conviction calls us to a different kind of freedom. It invites us to live without needing constant validation. It frees us from the exhausting task of curating an image. It allows us to stand where we stand, not because it is popular, but because it is right. That kind of freedom is costly, but it is also deeply peaceful. There is a calm that comes from not having to pretend.

But this calm is only possible when we are willing to lose something.

Conviction may cost us certain friendships. Not because we stop loving people, but because not everyone wants to walk alongside someone who will not compromise. It may cost us professional opportunities. Not because we are incompetent, but because we refuse to celebrate what we believe is harmful. It may cost us social approval. Not because we are unkind, but because we are clear. These losses hurt. They are real. And they often come without applause.

Yet there is something far more painful than losing approval. It is losing yourself.

When we betray our own convictions, even in small ways, something inside us fractures. We feel it. We become restless, uneasy, spiritually tired. We sense that we are not living in alignment with what we claim to believe. That dissonance creates a quiet misery. We may look successful on the outside, but inside we know something is wrong. Integrity has been traded for comfort, and comfort is a poor substitute for peace.

God never calls His people to live divided lives. He calls them to wholeness. He calls them to live with their inner and outer worlds aligned. Conviction makes that possible. It brings belief and behavior back into harmony. It creates a life that is honest, even when it is hard.

The world will tell us that conviction is rigid, intolerant, or outdated. But in reality, conviction is what makes real love possible. Without truth, love has no direction. Without boundaries, compassion has no shape. Conviction does not exist to exclude people. It exists to point them toward what is real, what is good, and what leads to life.

When we surrender conviction, we do not become more loving. We become more confused. We begin to affirm things that harm people while calling it kindness. We begin to celebrate choices that lead to emptiness while calling it freedom. And the people we claim to love are left without a map.

Conviction gives us a map.

It tells us where we are.

It tells us where we are going.

And it tells us when we have gone off course.

To carry conviction is to carry responsibility. It means being willing to be misunderstood for the sake of clarity. It means being willing to lose some things in order to protect something greater. It means trusting that God's truth is worth more than the world's approval.

Every believer must eventually face this question:

What am I willing to lose in order to remain faithful?

Because in the end, conviction will always demand payment.

The only choice is whether we pay it willingly…

or whether we pay it later through regret.

The Strength That Comes from Standing

Conviction does more than demand sacrifice—it produces strength. When a person chooses to stand for what is true, even when it costs them something, something solid begins to form inside. Integrity becomes more than a word. It becomes a backbone. The soul becomes anchored, no longer drifting with every shift in opinion or pressure.

This is why those who live by conviction often appear calmer in chaos. They are not constantly negotiating who they are. They know. They have settled the question of allegiance. That clarity creates stability. When storms come—criticism, rejection, uncertainty—they may feel the impact, but they do not lose their footing.

Standing for truth also sharpens perception. When you are no longer trying to please everyone, you begin to see more clearly. You can recognize manipulation, fear tactics, and false narratives because you are no longer invested in being approved by them. Conviction clears the fog. It allows you to live from a place of honesty rather than anxiety.

This kind of strength is contagious. People are drawn to those who know who they are. In a world filled with uncertainty, conviction looks like confidence—even when it is quiet. Others may not agree, but they respect the steadiness. That respect opens doors for deeper conversations and genuine influence.

God uses people who stand. Not because they are perfect, but because they are faithful. When we choose conviction over convenience, we become instruments through which truth can move. Even small acts of courage create ripples. Even a single voice can break the silence.

Standing is not always loud.

But it is always powerful.

When Conviction Becomes a Witness

When someone chooses to live by conviction, their life becomes a message. Not a speech, not a slogan, but a living testimony. People may argue with words, but they struggle to dismiss a life that is consistent, courageous, and grounded. In a world full of shifting identities and borrowed beliefs, someone who knows who they are stands out.

This is one of the great paradoxes of conviction: although it often leads to resistance, it also creates trust. People may not agree with you, but they can sense when you are real. They can tell when you are not playing a role or trying to win approval. That authenticity is rare, and it draws attention. Even those who oppose what you believe are often quietly impacted by how you live it.

Conviction gives faith credibility. It shows that belief is not just something you hold, but something that holds you. When people see someone remain faithful under pressure, it forces them to reconsider what they assume about Christianity. It disrupts the caricature of faith as weak, shallow, or merely traditional. A life of integrity tells a different story.

This is especially powerful in moments of suffering or loss. When someone who lives by conviction walks through hardship without collapsing, their faith becomes visible. It becomes tangible. Others begin to wonder what kind of strength could sustain a person through that. That curiosity opens hearts in ways that arguments never could.

Conviction also creates boundaries that protect relationships. When people know where you stand, they know what to expect. They may not always like it, but they respect it. Clarity reduces confusion. It prevents the slow erosion of trust that comes from inconsistency. When faith is lived honestly, it creates a kind of relational stability that is deeply attractive.

This does not mean conviction makes life easy. It often makes it harder. But it also makes it more meaningful. It gives weight to decisions. It gives purpose to sacrifice. It turns ordinary choices into acts of faith. And over time, those choices form a life that speaks louder than any debate.

In a culture saturated with noise, a life of conviction becomes a signal. It cuts through the chaos. It reminds people that there is something solid beneath all the uncertainty. Even those who are not ready to believe are often grateful to see someone who does.

God has always used faithful lives as His most persuasive argument. Not perfection, but persistence. Not performance, but obedience. When believers stand with quiet courage, they become beacons in a dark landscape.

Conviction does not force belief.

But it invites attention.

And in that attention, truth has a chance to be seen.

Choosing What Will Define You

Every person eventually reaches a moment when belief becomes a decision rather than a feeling. Up to that point, faith can exist comfortably in the background. It can be something we agree with, admire, or even love. But when truth collides with pressure, faith steps out of theory and into reality. We must choose whether it will remain an idea or become the defining force of our lives.

Conviction is what moves faith from the private to the public, from the internal to the embodied. It is the moment when belief becomes visible. And once belief is visible, it becomes vulnerable. People can respond to it. They can challenge it. They can resist it. That is why so many prefer a quiet faith. A hidden belief cannot be questioned. But a hidden belief also cannot change anything.

The world does not need more invisible Christians. It needs people whose lives point to something higher than convenience and comfort. When conviction shapes our decisions, it reshapes how we spend our time, how we speak, how we treat others, and how we respond to pressure. It becomes a compass that guides us through complexity. Without it, we drift.

What we choose to stand for becomes what we are known for. Silence may protect us for a season, but it also defines us. When we repeatedly avoid truth, we train ourselves to live cautiously. Over time, we become smaller, quieter, more careful. Conviction does the opposite. It expands us. It calls us into a larger life—one that is anchored in something greater than approval.

This is not a call to arrogance or hostility. It is a call to clarity. To know what you believe and why you believe it. To live in a way that reflects that belief, even when it costs something. That cost may be emotional. It may be social. It may be practical. But whatever it is, it is always outweighed by the peace that comes from integrity.

God does not ask His people to be perfect. He asks them to be faithful. Faithfulness means showing up when it would be easier to withdraw. It means speaking when it would be safer to stay quiet. It means choosing truth even when the world insists that truth is optional. These choices may not be celebrated, but they are never wasted.

A life shaped by conviction becomes a quiet force for good. It pushes back against lies simply by existing. It challenges confusion by offering clarity. It invites others to reconsider what they have accepted without question. This is how change begins—not with outrage, but with courage.

In the end, the question is not whether conviction will cost you something. It will. The question is whether you are willing to let it define you. A life built on conviction is not the easiest life, but it is the truest one. And in a world desperate for something real, that truth becomes a gift.

When believers choose conviction, they do more than protect their own faith. They create space for others to find theirs. They become living invitations to a deeper way of living. And in that invitation, hope is quietly born.

PRAYER

Father,

Give us hearts that choose truth even when it is costly. When fear whispers that silence is safer, remind us that obedience is stronger.

Shape us into people whose lives reflect what we believe, not just what we say. Let our conviction be rooted in love and guided by Your truth. In Jesus' name, Amen.

REFLECTION

1. 1.Where have I felt pressure to stay silent about what I believe?

2. 2.What fears most often keep me from living with greater conviction?

3. 3.How might my life look different if I chose truth over comfort more consistently?

CHALLENGE

This week, identify one place where you have been avoiding a difficult truth. Choose to respond with honesty and grace instead. Let it be a small but meaningful step toward becoming someone whose faith is visible, not hidden.

13

BUILDING A FAITH VANGUARD

A movement is born when people stop waiting for permission to live what they believe. Faith Vanguard is not an idea meant to be admired from a distance. It is a call to action for those who are no longer willing to let conviction stay quiet. It exists because a generation has realized that survival is not enough. We are called to build.

For too long, many believers have lived as if faith were something private and optional. Something that belonged safely in the heart but not boldly in the world. But faith that never steps outside the heart cannot change anything. A Faith Vanguard begins when belief becomes embodied — when people decide that truth will not only be held, but lived.

This does not require perfection. It requires courage. It requires the willingness to align everyday choices with eternal truth. In families, this means raising children who know why they believe. In communities, it means creating spaces where honesty and accountability are normal. In workplaces, it means carrying integrity into environments that reward compromise. Everywhere a believer stands, they bring something different with them.

A Faith Vanguard is not formed through noise. It is formed through consistency. When people live with conviction day after day, they create a quiet counterculture. Their values become visible. Their priorities become clear. And in a world hungry for something real, that visibility becomes a beacon.

This movement is not about controlling others. It is about governing ourselves. It is about choosing truth over trends, obedience over ease, and faithfulness over fear. When enough people make those choices together, the environment around them begins to shift. What was once considered normal starts to feel hollow. What was once considered radical starts to feel right.

Faith Vanguard is not built by institutions.

It is built by people.

People who pray when it would be easier to worry.

People who speak when it would be safer to stay quiet.

People who stand when others choose to drift.

The future will not belong to those who blend in.

It will belong to those who build.

How a Faith Vanguard Takes Shape

A Faith Vanguard is not created by a single event, a viral moment, or a powerful speech. It is formed slowly, through the steady accumulation of obedience. Long before a movement becomes visible, it becomes rooted. Long before it gains influence, it gains integrity. The people who become part of a Faith Vanguard are not waiting for ideal conditions. They are responding to an inner calling that tells them truth must be lived, not merely believed.

Every great movement in history has followed this pattern. It begins when a small number of people decide that convenience is no longer acceptable. They become uncomfortable with compromise. They feel the tension between what is and what should be. And instead of numbing that tension, they lean into it. They let it reshape how they think, speak, and act. That is where transformation begins.

A Faith Vanguard takes shape first in the private lives of believers. Before it ever becomes public, it becomes personal. People begin to pray differently. Not out of habit, but out of hunger. They open Scripture not to confirm what they already think, but to be changed. They start paying attention to where their lives do not align with what they claim to believe. And they begin to make adjustments, even when those adjustments are uncomfortable.

This is the invisible work that gives a movement its strength. When faith is practiced in private, it gains power in public. Conviction grows when it is exercised. Just as muscles become strong through resistance, belief becomes strong through obedience. A Faith Vanguard is built by people who are willing to do the unseen work of spiritual discipline.

As this inner alignment deepens, it naturally begins to affect relationships. People who are serious about their faith start seeking others who are serious as well. They recognize one another through shared values and shared courage. Conversations become deeper. Confessions become more honest. Prayers become more fervent. These relationships form the connective tissue of a movement. They create a network of trust that allows truth to flow freely.

This kind of community is not built on comfort. It is built on commitment. It is where people are known, not just welcomed. It is where weaknesses are addressed, not hidden. It is where growth is expected, not optional. A Faith Vanguard is sustained by these kinds of relationships because they produce people who are resilient, accountable, and strong.

As this network grows, it begins to change how people approach every part of life. Faith is no longer something reserved for church buildings. It becomes something that informs decisions at work, at home, and in public. Believers start asking different questions. Instead of "What is easiest?" they ask, "What is right?" Instead of "What will people think?" they ask, "What honors God?"

This shift has ripple effects. Families begin to change. Parents become more intentional. Children grow up seeing faith lived, not just spoken. Workplaces feel the presence of integrity. Communities feel the presence of people who care deeply about what is true and good. These changes may be subtle at first, but they are real.

A Faith Vanguard grows not by conquest, but by example. People are drawn to clarity in a world of confusion. They are drawn to peace in a world of anxiety. They are drawn to integrity in a world of performance. When believers live with conviction and grace, others notice. They may not agree at first, but they cannot ignore what is different.

This is how a movement begins to spread. Not through pressure, but through presence. Not through force, but through faithfulness. As more people encounter lives that are anchored in truth, curiosity is awakened. Questions are asked. Conversations begin. And in those moments, the gospel finds room to breathe.

A Faith Vanguard takes shape wherever people decide that truth is worth living for. It is built by those who are willing to be different, not because they want to stand out, but because they want to stand firm. Over time, those lives come together. And together, they become something far greater than they ever could alone.

From Personal Conviction to Public Culture

A Faith Vanguard cannot remain only a collection of inspired individuals. If it does, it will never survive the passage of time. Individual conviction is powerful, but conviction alone does not build something that can outlast a generation. What allows belief to endure is culture — the shared patterns of life that carry truth forward even when the original voices are gone.

Every lasting movement in history understood this. They did not merely persuade people to agree; they formed people to live differently. Culture is what transforms belief into a way of being. It is the invisible structure that shapes how people speak, how they choose, how they raise their children, and how they respond when pressure comes. A Faith Vanguard must become more than a collection of voices. It must become a way of life.

This is why habits matter. What people repeatedly do becomes who they are. When prayer becomes normal, hearts become sensitive. When Scripture becomes central, minds become anchored. When truth is spoken honestly, integrity becomes expected. Over time, these practices create an environment where faith can grow deep roots. Shallow faith cannot survive in difficult seasons, but rooted faith can withstand storms.

A Faith Vanguard grows strong through spiritual discipline. Not discipline that is rigid or joyless, but discipline that is purposeful. These practices are not about earning favor with God. They are about creating space for transformation. When believers take responsibility for their inner lives, they become less reactive and more resilient. They begin to respond to the world from a place of clarity instead of fear.

As individuals are formed, families begin to change. Parents become more intentional. Homes become places where faith is discussed, not just assumed. Children grow up seeing what belief looks like when it is lived honestly. They learn that faith is not something you put on for special occasions, but something that shapes everyday decisions. This is how conviction is passed from one generation to the next.

When families change, communities follow. A Faith Vanguard does not withdraw from the world. It engages it with a different spirit. Believers bring patience into tense situations. They bring integrity into dishonest systems. They bring compassion into broken places. Over time, this consistent presence begins to influence the atmosphere. People notice when something feels different. They notice when a group of people lives by a higher standard without becoming harsh or self-righteous.

This is how public culture begins to shift. Not through domination, but through example. Not through shouting, but through steadiness. When people see lives marked by peace, clarity, and purpose, curiosity is awakened. Questions begin to form. Conversations open. And in those moments, truth finds a way in.

A Faith Vanguard also learns how to protect what it is building. Culture must be guarded if it is to remain healthy. Without clarity about values, a movement becomes vulnerable to confusion. Without accountability, it becomes vulnerable to compromise. A Faith Vanguard therefore creates spaces where people can grow, but also where they can be corrected when they drift. This is not about control. It is about care.

Healthy culture produces healthy leaders. When people are formed in an environment of truth and grace, they become capable of carrying responsibility. They are not driven by ego or ambition, but by a desire to serve. Over time, these leaders emerge naturally from the community. They are trusted because they have been tested. They are respected because they have been faithful.

This is how a movement becomes self-sustaining. It no longer depends on one voice or one personality. It becomes a network of people who share a vision and live by it. That network can endure opposition, adapt to change, and continue moving forward even when circumstances shift.

A Faith Vanguard is not built for a moment.

It is built for the future.

By forming culture rooted in truth, it ensures that the faith being lived today will still be alive tomorrow. It creates a bridge between generations. It provides a home for those who are searching. And it offers the world a glimpse of what life can look like when it is shaped by something greater than fear.

That is how personal conviction becomes a public force —

not through spectacle,

but through substance.

How a Movement Becomes a Force

A Faith Vanguard does not become powerful by accident. It becomes powerful when enough people choose to align their lives around something higher than themselves. This alignment is what transforms scattered conviction into collective strength. One person standing in truth is courageous. Many people standing together becomes unstoppable.

Every lasting movement follows this same pattern. It begins in hearts, but it must grow into systems. Not systems of control, but systems of continuity. Without them, even the strongest convictions fade when the people who held them grow tired or pass away. A Faith Vanguard must be built in a way that allows faith to outlive any single generation.

This is where depth becomes more important than numbers. Many movements chase size, but size without substance collapses under pressure. A Faith Vanguard chases faithfulness. It builds people who are anchored, disciplined, and clear about what they believe. When those people connect, something durable begins to form. They are not held together by hype, but by shared conviction.

Unity rooted in truth creates coherence. People no longer pull in different directions. They may have different gifts, personalities, and callings, but they are oriented toward the same center. That shared center gives the movement stability. It allows disagreement without division and diversity without dilution. When truth is the foundation, difference becomes a strength rather than a threat.

As this unity grows, so does trust. Trust is the currency of any movement. Without it, nothing lasting can be built. People must know that others will act with integrity, speak with honesty, and protect what is being formed. A Faith Vanguard builds this trust slowly, through consistency. People show up. They keep their word. They do what they say they will do. Over time, this reliability creates a culture of mutual respect.

With trust comes shared responsibility. The work no longer rests on a few. It is carried by many. Leadership becomes distributed. People step into roles not because they seek attention, but because they feel accountable to the mission. This creates resilience. When challenges arise, the movement does not collapse because it is not dependent on a single pillar. It is supported by a network.

As influence begins to grow, temptation follows. There will always be pressure to soften the message, to make it more acceptable, to trade depth for reach. Every movement that hopes to survive must face this test. A Faith Vanguard must decide whether it values truth more than applause. Growth that is purchased through compromise is not growth—it is erosion.

Faithfulness is what preserves the soul of a movement. When leaders refuse to bend to convenience, they protect the integrity of what is being built. That integrity gives the movement moral authority. People can sense when something is real. Even critics recognize consistency. Over time, that consistency becomes a source of influence that cannot be manufactured.

A Faith Vanguard also learns to think beyond the present moment. It begins to ask what will remain when today's leaders are gone. This is where legacy is formed. Schools, churches, networks, and communities become tools for transmission. They are not the heart of the movement, but they carry it forward. They ensure that truth does not have to be rediscovered by each new generation.

Legacy requires intention. It requires training new leaders. It requires teaching not just what to believe, but how to live. It requires creating spaces where faith can be practiced, tested, and strengthened. A Faith Vanguard invests in people because people are what carry the future.

Over time, a movement built this way becomes difficult to destroy. It is not dependent on one location or one personality. It is woven into the fabric of countless lives. Even when opposition comes, the movement endures because it is rooted in something deeper than popularity. It is rooted in truth.

A Faith Vanguard does not need to dominate to make an impact. It influences by being present. It shapes culture by living differently. It challenges assumptions simply by existing. In a world full of noise, it becomes a steady, unwavering signal.

This is how a movement becomes a force.

Not through power grabs,

but through faithful persistence.

Not through control,

but through conviction.

When enough people live with clarity and courage, they change the landscape around them. They build something that lasts. And in that legacy, faith finds a home that the future cannot easily erase.

The Responsibility of Those Who Build

When a movement begins to take shape, it creates more than opportunity—it creates responsibility. A Faith Vanguard is not simply a gathering of like-minded people. It is a living structure that influences families, communities, and futures. Those who participate in building it are not just followers; they become stewards of something far larger than themselves.

Stewardship changes how we see our faith. It reminds us that what we have been given is not only for our own growth, but for the benefit of others. Conviction is not meant to be hoarded. It is meant to be shared, modeled, and passed on. When believers begin to understand this, their perspective shifts. Faith stops being something they consume and becomes something they contribute.

This sense of responsibility matures people. It forces them to move beyond spiritual infancy. They begin to think not only about what they need, but about what others need from them. They ask how their words, actions, and choices shape the environment around them. They recognize that leadership is not a title—it is influence. And everyone, whether they realize it or not, is influencing someone.

A Faith Vanguard must be built by people who take that influence seriously. Parents influence children. Friends influence friends. Mentors influence those who are watching them. Every life becomes a testimony, either pointing toward truth or pulling others away from it. When this reality is understood, it produces a deeper level of care and intentionality.

Responsibility also means guarding the spirit of the movement. As Faith Vanguard grows, it will attract people with many different motivations. Some will come seeking truth. Others will come seeking belonging. Some will come with wounds that need healing. Others will come with agendas. Leaders and members alike must learn to discern these differences with wisdom and grace. The goal is not to exclude people, but to protect the heart of what is being built.

This is why humility is essential. A movement built on pride will eventually collapse under its own weight. A movement built on service will endure. Those who build Faith Vanguard must resist the temptation to see themselves as superior or enlightened. They are not chosen because they are better. They are chosen because they are willing. Willing to stand. Willing to serve. Willing to sacrifice.

As responsibility grows, so does the need for wisdom. Decisions must be made with care. Conflicts must be handled with honesty and compassion. Vision must be protected without becoming rigid. A Faith Vanguard must remain rooted in truth while staying open to the leading of God. This balance is what allows a movement to remain both strong and alive.

There will be moments of disagreement. There will be seasons of difficulty. There will be times when the path forward is not clear. These moments are not signs of failure. They are signs that something real is being built. Only what matters is ever tested.

Those who choose to build rather than drift will face pressure. But they will also experience the deep satisfaction that comes from being part of something that has meaning. They will know that their lives are contributing to something that will outlast them. That knowledge brings a quiet joy that no amount of comfort can replace.

A Faith Vanguard is not built by spectators.

It is built by servants.

People who are willing to carry weight.

People who are willing to invest time.

People who are willing to put their faith into action.

This is the kind of responsibility that changes a generation. It creates leaders who are shaped by integrity. It forms communities that are grounded in truth. And it builds a future that is worth inheriting.

Raising a Generation That Can Carry It

A Faith Vanguard that does not think generationally is building something temporary. Movements that fail to prepare the next generation do not fade because they lack passion—they fade because they lack continuity. If truth is not passed on, it must be rediscovered. And what must be rediscovered is often distorted.

Raising a generation that can carry Faith Vanguard forward begins with intention. Children and young believers do not inherit conviction by default. They absorb what they see modeled. They learn what matters by watching what adults prioritize. If faith is treated as optional, they will treat it as optional. If it is lived with courage and consistency, they will come to see it as essential.

This is why families matter so deeply. Homes are the first training ground for belief. Long before someone chooses what they believe, they watch how belief is lived. When parents pray, forgive, and speak truth, they teach far more than words ever could. A Faith Vanguard grows strong when households become places where faith is practiced daily, not just discussed weekly.

Communities also play a critical role. Young people need more than their parents. They need mentors. They need examples of adults who have walked with God through struggle, doubt, and hardship. When young believers see faith carried through adversity, it becomes credible. It stops feeling fragile and starts feeling strong.

A Faith Vanguard must therefore invest in relationships that bridge generations. Wisdom must flow downward. Energy must flow upward. When these streams meet, a powerful exchange occurs. The old offer perspective. The young bring vision. Together, they create something neither could build alone.

Education is also part of this process. Not just formal schooling, but spiritual formation. Young people must be taught how to think, not just what to think. They need to understand why truth matters, how to recognize falsehood, and how to stand when pressure comes. This kind of formation equips them not just to believe, but to lead.

As a new generation rises, the movement must be willing to entrust them with real responsibility. Nothing forms character like being trusted. When young leaders are given space to serve, make decisions, and even make mistakes, they grow. A Faith Vanguard that refuses to release control will eventually choke its own future.

Passing on faith is not about preserving a museum.

It is about planting a living forest.

Each generation must take what was given and grow it further. When that happens, Faith Vanguard becomes something that continues to breathe, adapt, and expand without losing its core.

The goal is not to keep things the same.

The goal is to keep them true.

And when truth is faithfully carried forward, it becomes a gift that no generation has to live without.

Living as a Vanguard in the World

A Faith Vanguard does not exist to withdraw from the world, but to walk within it with purpose. Believers are not called to hide from culture or to isolate themselves from society. They are called to engage it with clarity, integrity, and love. The challenge is not whether we will be influenced by the world, but whether we will influence it.

Living as part of a Faith Vanguard means carrying your convictions into every space you enter. It means letting faith shape how you speak, how you work, how you respond to conflict, and how you treat others. These are not small things. They are the places where belief becomes visible. A life lived with intention becomes a quiet testimony to something greater.

This kind of living requires discernment. Not every opportunity is worth pursuing. Not every voice deserves to be followed. A Faith Vanguard must learn to recognize what aligns with its values and what undermines them. This does not mean rejecting everything unfamiliar. It means approaching everything with wisdom. Truth gives us a lens through which to see the world more clearly.

When believers live this way, they bring stability into unstable environments. They become people others can trust. They become known for honesty, fairness, and compassion. These qualities open doors. They create influence that cannot be manufactured. In a world hungry for authenticity, lives of conviction stand out.

A Faith Vanguard also understands that opposition is inevitable. Standing for truth will sometimes create tension. But tension is not always a sign of wrongdoing. Often it is a sign that something meaningful is happening. When faith challenges falsehood, discomfort follows. But in that discomfort, growth becomes possible.

Living as a Vanguard means choosing courage over ease. It means being willing to be misunderstood for the sake of being faithful. It means holding to truth even when it costs something. These choices are rarely dramatic, but they are deeply powerful. Over time, they shape a life that is strong, steady, and real.

The world is watching.

Not to find perfection,

but to find authenticity.

And when people see faith lived honestly, it invites them to look again at what they may have dismissed. That is how a Faith Vanguard fulfills its purpose—not by retreating from the world, but by being fully present within it.

What We Are Actually Building

A Faith Vanguard is not just a response to what is broken. It is a vision for what can be restored. While much of the world is focused on what is being lost, a Vanguard is focused on what can be built. It refuses to live in despair or nostalgia. It chooses to invest in the future with faith.

What is being built is not merely an organization. It is a way of life rooted in truth, shaped by discipline, and sustained by community. It is a network of people who know what they believe and are willing to live it. It is a culture that values integrity over image, faithfulness over fame, and obedience over ease.

This kind of culture becomes a shelter in a chaotic world. People who are tired of confusion find clarity. People who are weary of shallow living find depth. People who are searching for meaning find a path. A Faith Vanguard becomes a place where faith is not diluted but strengthened, not hidden but honored.

Building something like this takes time. It requires patience, sacrifice, and perseverance. It demands that people continue to show up when enthusiasm fades and challenges arise. But what is built through faith endures beyond circumstances. It becomes something that can support others when they are struggling.

The world may not always celebrate what is being built. But it will be shaped by it. Every life that is transformed becomes part of the foundation. Every family that is strengthened becomes part of the structure. Every community that is touched becomes part of the legacy.

A Faith Vanguard is built one life at a time.

One choice at a time.

One act of obedience at a time.

And as those pieces come together, something far greater than any individual begins to emerge. A future grounded in truth. A generation equipped to stand. A legacy that will outlive us all.

PRAYER

Father,

Thank You for calling us to build and not retreat. Give us the courage to live what we believe, the wisdom to lead with humility, and the strength to carry what You are creating through us. Let our lives become foundations for truth, faith, and hope for generations to come. In Jesus' name, Amen.

REFLECTION

1. In what ways is God calling me to be more intentional about how I live my faith?

2. Where have I been hesitant to step into responsibility or leadership?

3. What kind of legacy do I want my life to leave behind?

CHALLENGE

This week, take one concrete step toward building rather than drifting. Invest time in a relationship, begin a new spiritual habit, or commit to serving in a way that strengthens your community. Let your faith become something that builds a future, not just something that comforts the present.

14

BECOMING THE LEADERS THE FUTURE NEEDS

Every generation is shaped by the leaders it produces. Not just those with titles, but those with influence. Families rise or fall based on leadership. Communities thrive or fracture based on leadership. Nations move forward or decay based on leadership. The question is not whether leadership matters. The question is what kind of leaders will be formed.

A Faith Vanguard cannot be sustained by passive believers. It requires people who are willing to step forward, take responsibility, and guide others with integrity. Leadership in this sense is not about power. It is about service. It is about being willing to carry weight so that others can grow.

True leadership begins in the unseen places. It starts with character long before it shows up in public. A leader is formed by how they treat people when no one is watching, how they respond when things go wrong, and how they handle success when it comes. These quiet choices determine whether someone will build something healthy or simply gather attention.

The future needs leaders who are anchored in truth. Leaders who are not swayed by every opinion or pressured by every trend. Leaders who can listen without losing clarity and engage without losing conviction. This kind of steadiness is rare, but it is exactly what creates trust.

A Faith Vanguard exists to cultivate this kind of leadership. It forms people who know who they are and why they stand where they stand. When leaders are rooted, the people they serve feel secure. And when people feel secure, they are free to grow.

Leadership is not reserved for the few. Every believer is called to lead in some way. In a home. In a workplace. In a community. Wherever influence exists, leadership is already happening. The only question is whether it is happening with intention.

A Faith Vanguard does not wait for the world to define leadership.

It shapes leaders who can define the world.

What True Leadership Is Built On

Leadership that lasts is not built on charisma, position, or popularity. It is built on character. Titles can be given. Influence must be earned. A Faith Vanguard does not produce leaders who seek attention—it forms leaders who seek responsibility. These are the kind of people who step forward when something needs to be done, not because they want recognition, but because they feel accountable.

Character is what holds a leader steady when pressure comes. Anyone can lead when things are easy. It is far harder to lead when decisions are costly, when people are disappointed, and when the right choice is not the comfortable one. This is where true leadership is revealed. Not in how loudly someone speaks, but in how faithfully they stand.

A leader shaped by faith understands that authority is not something to be used for personal gain. It is something to be stewarded for the good of others. This changes everything. When leadership becomes service, it creates environments where people can flourish. Instead of fear, there is trust. Instead of competition, there is cooperation. Instead of control, there is care.

A Faith Vanguard must therefore be deeply invested in forming leaders from the inside out. Skills matter, but they are not enough. Vision matters, but without integrity it becomes manipulation. Wisdom matters, but without humility it becomes arrogance. True leadership requires all of these to be grounded in something deeper: truth.

Truth gives leaders a compass. It tells them where they are, where they are going, and when they have gone off course. Without it, leadership becomes reactive. With it, leadership becomes intentional. People can sense the difference. They are drawn to leaders who know what they stand for and live accordingly.

Leadership also requires the courage to make difficult decisions. There will be moments when pleasing everyone is impossible. A leader must be willing to choose what is right over what is popular. This does not mean being harsh or unkind. It means being clear. Clarity is one of the greatest gifts a leader can offer. It allows people to know where they stand and what is expected.

A Faith Vanguard produces leaders who are not afraid of conflict, but who do not seek it either. They approach disagreement with wisdom and grace. They listen carefully, speak honestly, and remain grounded in truth. This balance creates environments where people feel both safe and challenged.

As leaders grow, so does their influence. They begin to shape not only individuals, but cultures. Families, organizations, and communities reflect the values of those who lead them. When leaders are formed in truth and humility, the places they serve become healthier. This is how a Faith Vanguard changes the world—not through domination, but through transformation.

True leadership is not about being above others.

It is about standing for something so clearly that others are inspired to rise.

Forming Leaders Who Can Be Trusted

Trust is the foundation of all real leadership. Without it, influence collapses into control. People may comply out of fear, but they will never follow with their hearts. A Faith Vanguard cannot be built on compliance. It must be built on credibility. Leaders must become people whose words carry weight because their lives consistently back them up.

Trust is not created through image. It is created through repeated integrity. It grows when people see a leader make difficult decisions for the sake of what is right rather than what is convenient. It deepens when someone admits mistakes instead of hiding them. It becomes unshakable when a leader remains faithful even when there is no reward. These are the moments that shape reputation, even when no one thinks they are being watched.

A Faith Vanguard requires leaders who understand that leadership is not performance. It is stewardship. Every influence given must be handled carefully. Every relationship carries responsibility. Every decision shapes the environment for others. When leaders live with this awareness, they become protective of the people they serve. They are careful with their words. They are slow to judge. They are quick to listen. They lead not from ego, but from accountability.

This kind of leadership creates safety. People feel free to be honest. They feel safe to admit weakness. They feel secure enough to grow. When fear is removed from a community, learning accelerates. People take risks. They try new things. They step into callings they might otherwise avoid. Trust becomes the soil where potential can take root.

In a Faith Vanguard, leaders must also be willing to be known. Transparency is not optional. Hidden lives eventually produce hidden damage. Leaders who are open about their struggles, their doubts, and their growth create an environment where authenticity is normal. When leaders model vulnerability, others follow. When leaders hide, others pretend. A culture of honesty begins at the top.

Accountability must also be built into leadership. No one should lead in isolation. Every leader must have people who can challenge them, correct them, and protect them from themselves. Power without accountability is dangerous. A Faith Vanguard that wants to endure must design structures that prevent any one person from becoming untouchable.

This is how trust is preserved. People do not have to wonder whether leaders are acting in their own interest or in the interest of the mission. The system itself makes integrity visible. When trust is protected this way, the movement becomes strong enough to survive pressure, growth, and even failure.

Leadership also requires discernment. Not everyone who wants influence should have it. Not every gifted person is ready to lead. Character must always come before competence. A Faith Vanguard must be willing to say no to those who seek authority for the wrong reasons. This may slow growth in the short term, but it preserves health in the long term.

Leaders who can be trusted are patient. They are willing to wait for people to mature. They understand that formation takes time. They do not rush others into positions they are not ready to carry. Instead, they invest, mentor, and prepare. This produces leaders who are steady rather than flashy, rooted rather than reactive.

Over time, a Faith Vanguard becomes known not for its charisma, but for its credibility. People know that what is said will be done. They know that promises will be kept. They know that truth will not be sacrificed for convenience. That reputation becomes one of the movement's greatest assets.

A world full of broken trust is desperate for leaders who can be believed.

When a Faith Vanguard produces leaders who are consistent, accountable, and humble, it becomes a place where people can rest, grow, and serve without fear. That is how real leadership changes lives. And that is how a movement becomes something worth following.

The Weight and Privilege of Influence

Influence is one of the most powerful forces in the world, and one of the least understood. It moves people, shapes cultures, and determines futures, often without anyone noticing it happening. A Faith Vanguard does not treat influence lightly, because it knows that every life it touches will be shaped by what it models. Leadership is never neutral. It is always forming something, even when it is quiet.

Every leader carries a wake behind them. Their words, choices, and reactions leave traces in the hearts and minds of those who follow. When leaders are careless, that wake becomes destructive. When they are faithful, it becomes life-giving. This is why leadership is not about visibility; it is about responsibility. The more people who are watching you, the more carefully you must live.

Many people are drawn to leadership because they want to be seen. A Faith Vanguard forms leaders who are willing to be accountable. These are not the same. Being seen brings attention. Being accountable brings weight. Leaders who understand this do not seek influence for its own sake. They accept it because they feel called to serve something greater than themselves.

The weight of influence means that leaders must be willing to sacrifice comfort. They cannot always say what they want. They cannot always do what is easiest. They must consider how their actions will affect those who are watching. This does not mean living in fear. It means living in awareness. A Faith Vanguard leader knows that every moment is an opportunity to either strengthen or weaken the people around them.

Influence also demands integrity. A leader who says one thing and lives another will eventually fracture trust. Hypocrisy erodes credibility, even when it is subtle. Over time, people begin to feel that something is off. They may not be able to name it, but they sense it. A Faith Vanguard cannot afford that kind of erosion. It must be built on leaders whose lives align with their message.

This alignment is what creates moral authority. Authority that comes from position can be taken away. Authority that comes from integrity cannot. People choose to follow leaders they respect, not just leaders they are required to obey. In a Faith Vanguard, leadership is invited by example, not imposed by force.

With influence also comes the responsibility to protect others. Leaders must be attentive to the emotional, spiritual, and relational health of those they serve. They must notice when someone is struggling. They must intervene when harm is being done. They must create spaces where people feel safe to grow. This is not weakness. It is stewardship.

A Faith Vanguard leader understands that power can easily become dangerous if it is not held with humility. They resist the temptation to control. They invite feedback. They remain teachable. They know that being wrong is not a threat—it is an opportunity to grow. This posture keeps a movement healthy and prevents it from becoming rigid or abusive.

Influence also creates moments of loneliness. Leaders often carry burdens that others do not see. They make decisions that not everyone will understand. They stand in tension between competing needs. A Faith Vanguard prepares its leaders for this reality. It teaches them to draw strength from God and from trusted relationships, rather than from applause.

Despite its weight, influence is also a profound privilege. To shape lives, to encourage growth, to witness transformation—these are gifts few experiences can match. A leader who sees someone step into their calling, overcome fear, or deepen their faith is witnessing something sacred. That is the reward of faithful leadership.

A Faith Vanguard exists to cultivate leaders who honor this privilege. Leaders who do not take influence for granted. Leaders who recognize that every person they serve is someone's child, someone's hope, someone's future. This awareness brings both tenderness and resolve.

When influence is carried with humility, courage, and love, it becomes one of the greatest forces for good in the world. It builds families. It heals communities. It preserves truth.

That is the kind of influence a Faith Vanguard is called to wield.

Not to elevate itself, but to lift others.

The Courage to Lead When It Would Be Easier to Follow

True leadership reveals itself most clearly when the path forward is not popular. When consensus disappears, when opinions clash, and when pressure mounts, leaders must decide whether they will be guided by conviction or by convenience. A Faith Vanguard exists because too many people have been willing to follow when they were meant to stand. Leadership requires the courage to be different.

The world is not short on voices. It is short on courage. Trends move quickly, and they bring with them the expectation that everyone will keep up. But a leader who is always chasing what is new will never be rooted in what is true. A Faith Vanguard forms leaders who are willing to pause, to discern, and to choose wisely even when the choice is costly.

This courage does not come from stubbornness. It comes from clarity. Leaders who know what they believe are not easily shaken by what others think. They can listen without losing their footing. They can engage without surrendering their values. This steadiness becomes a source of strength for those who follow. People do not need leaders who agree with everyone. They need leaders who can see clearly and guide faithfully.

Courageous leadership also requires the willingness to bear misunderstanding. Not everyone will celebrate a leader who chooses truth over popularity. There will be moments when decisions are questioned, motives are doubted, and sacrifices are unseen. A Faith Vanguard leader must be prepared for this. They must be willing to be misinterpreted if it means being faithful.

This kind of courage is often quiet. It does not always make headlines. It is found in conversations behind closed doors, in choices made when no one is watching, and in commitments kept when enthusiasm fades. Over time, these quiet acts of courage build a reputation that speaks louder than any speech ever could.

Leaders who stand in this way create environments where others feel safe to be honest. They show that it is possible to live with integrity without becoming harsh. They model how to disagree without becoming divided. This creates communities that are strong enough to handle complexity without losing unity.

A Faith Vanguard also teaches leaders how to navigate fear. Fear is not the enemy. It is a signal. It tells us when something matters. Courage does not mean the absence of fear. It means choosing to act in spite of it. Leaders who understand this do not wait for fear to disappear before they move. They move because the call is greater.

As leaders practice this courage, they become more confident in their calling. They begin to trust that God is at work even when outcomes are uncertain. This trust frees them from the need to control everything. They can lead with open hands, knowing that faithfulness is more important than success.

The courage to lead also includes the courage to rest. Leaders who never stop eventually burn out. A Faith Vanguard values sustainability. It teaches leaders to care for their own souls so they can continue to care for others. Rest is not a sign of weakness. It is a sign of wisdom.

When leaders choose courage over conformity, they create a ripple effect. Others are emboldened. Voices that were quiet begin to speak. Convictions that were hidden begin to surface. This is how a movement grows—not through force, but through example.

A Faith Vanguard needs leaders who are willing to step forward when it would be easier to blend in.

Leaders who will speak when it would be safer to stay silent.

Leaders who will stand when others choose to drift.

That courage becomes the backbone of everything that follows.

The Inner Life That Sustains Outer Leadership

Leadership that endures is not sustained by talent or momentum. It is sustained by the inner life. A Faith Vanguard understands that what happens inside a leader will always determine what happens through them. When the inner world is neglected, the outer work eventually collapses. But when the inner life is tended with care, leadership becomes strong, steady, and resilient.

The greatest threat to a leader is not opposition. It is drift. Drift happens when the pace of life grows faster than the pace of reflection. When prayer becomes hurried. When Scripture becomes optional. When silence disappears. A leader may still be effective for a time, but slowly their clarity fades. Decisions become reactive instead of rooted. Discernment becomes dull. Fatigue begins to creep in. A Faith Vanguard teaches leaders to guard against this slow erosion.

Spiritual disciplines are not spiritual decorations. They are the infrastructure of leadership. Prayer is where leaders learn to listen before they speak. Scripture is where they learn to see before they decide. Worship is where they remember who they are and who God is. These practices recalibrate the heart. They keep ambition from becoming idolatry and activity from becoming escape.

Leaders who neglect their inner life often compensate with control. When they no longer feel grounded, they try to manage everything around them. They become anxious, defensive, and brittle. A Faith Vanguard calls leaders to a different posture. One of surrender. One of trust. One that allows God to carry what no human was meant to bear alone.

The inner life also shapes how leaders treat people. When a leader is emotionally and spiritually healthy, they respond with patience. They listen without rushing. They correct without cruelty. They forgive without bitterness. But when the inner life is strained, small frustrations become large conflicts. People begin to feel like obstacles rather than partners. This is why self-awareness is not optional for leaders—it is essential.

A Faith Vanguard trains leaders to know themselves. To recognize their own triggers. To understand their own weaknesses. To seek help when they need it. This kind of honesty creates safety. It gives others permission to be real. And real communities are the ones that last.

There will be seasons when leadership feels heavy. When criticism is loud. When progress is slow. When doubts creep in. In those moments, the inner life becomes the anchor. It reminds leaders why they began. It reconnects them to their calling. It restores perspective when everything feels overwhelming.

The world often celebrates leaders who are always busy. A Faith Vanguard celebrates leaders who are always becoming. Becoming more humble. More wise. More rooted in truth. More attuned to God. This is the kind of growth that makes leadership sustainable.

Outer success without inner depth is fragile.

Outer influence without inner integrity is dangerous.

Outer leadership without inner life is hollow.

A Faith Vanguard builds leaders who are deep enough to carry the weight of what they are called to lead. And because of that depth, they are able to stand when others fall, to remain steady when others sway, and to continue building when others grow weary.

That is how leadership becomes not just effective, but faithful.

Leading in a World That Pushes Back

Any leader who stands for truth will eventually feel resistance. Not because they are doing something wrong, but because they are doing something real. A Faith Vanguard is not built in environments of comfort. It is built in environments of pressure. When a leader chooses conviction over convenience, the world responds.

We live in a culture that is deeply uncomfortable with moral clarity. It prefers ambiguity because ambiguity allows everyone to be right. But leaders who know what they believe create friction simply by existing. They expose contradictions. They challenge assumptions. They refuse to call darkness light just because it is popular. That refusal makes them targets.

Opposition does not always arrive in obvious forms. Sometimes it comes as mockery. Sometimes it comes as misunderstanding. Sometimes it comes as quiet exclusion. Leaders may find doors closing, opportunities disappearing, or relationships becoming strained. These moments test more than patience—they test identity. A leader must decide whether their sense of worth comes from approval or from calling.

A Faith Vanguard prepares its leaders for this. It teaches them that resistance is not proof of failure. Often, it is proof of faithfulness. When truth enters a space that has been shaped by compromise, discomfort is inevitable. Light always exposes what darkness prefers to hide.

Leading through resistance requires emotional strength. It is easy to become defensive when criticized. It is tempting to grow bitter when misrepresented. But leaders who allow resentment to take root begin to lead from woundedness instead of wisdom. A Faith Vanguard calls leaders to a higher road. One that responds with clarity rather than retaliation, and courage rather than contempt.

This does not mean being passive. It means being principled. Leaders must learn how to speak with both firmness and grace. They must know when to confront and when to remain silent. They must be able to discern whether opposition is coming from misunderstanding or from hostility. That discernment protects both the leader and the community.

There will also be moments when resistance comes from within. Not everyone will agree with every decision. Even people who share the same faith will sometimes see things differently. A Faith Vanguard does not avoid these tensions. It navigates them with honesty. Leaders listen. They explain. They stay rooted in truth while remaining open to growth. This balance builds trust and prevents division.

One of the greatest dangers during resistance is discouragement. When progress feels slow and criticism is loud, leaders can begin to wonder if the effort is worth it. This is where perseverance becomes essential. Movements that last are not built by those who never struggle. They are built by those who refuse to quit.

A Faith Vanguard teaches its leaders to measure success differently. Not by applause, but by faithfulness. Not by popularity, but by integrity. Not by how many people agree, but by whether truth is being honored. This perspective allows leaders to remain steady even when the environment is unstable.

Resistance also reveals the depth of a leader's convictions. It forces them to decide what they are willing to sacrifice. Comfort? Reputation? Opportunity? The leaders who endure are those who have already settled that question. They know why they stand, and they know what they stand for.

When leaders walk through resistance with humility and courage, they become examples for others. They show that it is possible to live with conviction without becoming harsh. They demonstrate that strength and compassion are not opposites. They create a culture where people feel safe to be honest and brave enough to be faithful.

A Faith Vanguard does not promise an easy road.

It promises a meaningful one.

And leaders who walk it with integrity leave footprints that others can follow.

The Legacy of Faithful Leadership

Leadership is never just about the present. Every decision a leader makes is shaping the future, whether they realize it or not. A Faith Vanguard exists because faithful leadership creates ripples that move through generations. The choices made today become the foundations that tomorrow's leaders will stand on.

A leader who lives with conviction teaches others how to live with courage. A leader who leads with humility shows others how to serve. A leader who remains faithful through difficulty models endurance. These lessons are not taught in classrooms. They are taught through lives that are observed, remembered, and imitated.

This is how legacy is formed. It is not written in policies or speeches. It is written in people. When someone grows because of a leader's guidance, that growth becomes part of the leader's story. When a family is strengthened because of a leader's example, that strength becomes part of the leader's impact. Long after a leader's voice is gone, their influence continues to speak.

A Faith Vanguard aims to create this kind of legacy. It is not focused on short-term success, but on long-term faithfulness. Leaders are encouraged to think beyond their own lives. They are invited to consider what they are handing to the next generation. Not just resources, but values. Not just structures, but truth.

This perspective changes how leaders make decisions. They become more patient. More intentional. More careful with what they build and what they allow. They know that what they tolerate today will shape what others inherit tomorrow. That awareness brings both gravity and hope.

Faithful leadership does not guarantee ease. But it does guarantee meaning. A life spent building others, protecting truth, and standing with integrity is never wasted. Even when results are not immediately visible, something eternal is being formed.

A Faith Vanguard is built by leaders who understand this.

Leaders who are willing to invest in people rather than chase recognition.

Leaders who are willing to plant seeds they may never see grow.

That is the heart of faithful leadership.

And that is the legacy that will endure.

PRAYER

Father,

Thank You for calling us to lead with humility and courage. Shape our hearts so that we serve with integrity, speak with wisdom, and walk in truth. Teach us to carry the weight of influence with grace, and to use it to lift others rather than ourselves. Let our leadership reflect Your love and Your light. In Jesus' name, Amen.

. . .

REFLECTION

1. Where has God placed me in a position of influence right now?

2. How can I lead with greater humility and integrity in that space?

1. What kind of legacy do I want my leadership to leave behind?

CHALLENGE

This week, intentionally encourage or mentor someone who looks to you for guidance. Lead not through control, but through example. Let your faith be something others can see, not just something you feel.

15

THE FUTURE WE ARE CALLED TO BUILD

The future is not something we wait for. It is something we shape. Every generation inherits the results of the choices made before it, and every generation decides what the next will receive. A Faith Vanguard exists because the future is too important to leave to drift. We are called not just to believe, but to build something that will last.

Much of modern life is focused on the immediate. People chase what is fast, easy, and visible. But anything built quickly can also be lost quickly. Faith Vanguard is not interested in temporary impact. It is committed to enduring transformation. It is focused on creating a spiritual architecture that will hold when the storms of culture and history begin to press against it.

Building the future begins with vision. Vision is not imagination. It is seeing what could be and choosing to move toward it. It is the ability to look beyond current limitations and recognize what God is inviting us to become. A Faith Vanguard is a people who refuse to be defined by what is broken. They are defined by what can be restored.

This vision must be shared. A future cannot be built by one person alone. It requires many hands, many voices, and many hearts aligned around a common purpose. When people understand what they are building, they are willing to sacrifice for it. They are willing to endure discomfort. They are willing to invest time, energy, and love into something that may not bear fruit immediately.

A Faith Vanguard does not measure success by how many people are watching. It measures success by how many people are being formed. Are families growing stronger? Are communities becoming healthier? Are individuals becoming more grounded in truth? These are the signs that a future worth inheriting is being built.

Building the future also requires patience. Seeds do not grow overnight. Neither do movements. Faithfulness is often quiet and unseen, but it is never wasted. Every prayer, every act of service, every choice to stand in truth adds to the foundation. Over time, those small acts become something sturdy enough to support generations.

A Faith Vanguard is not afraid of the long road. It knows that what is worth building takes time. It is willing to work when no one is applauding. It is willing to keep going when progress feels slow. That perseverance is what turns vision into reality.

The future we are called to build is not just safer or stronger. It is truer. It is a future where faith is not fragile, where truth is not optional, and where people know who they are and why they stand where they do. It is a future where conviction and compassion walk hand in hand.

This is the work before us.

Not to survive.

But to build.

And every choice we make today becomes part of what tomorrow will inherit.

Laying Foundations That Will Last

. . .

A future that can endure is never built on impulse. It is built on intention. Long before a building rises, someone must decide where it will stand, how it will be supported, and what kind of weight it must be able to bear. A Faith Vanguard approaches the future the same way. It does not simply react to what is happening around it. It plans for what is coming.

Foundations are formed in places few people ever see. They are laid beneath the surface, in soil that must be prepared, cleared, and strengthened. In the same way, the future is shaped by unseen decisions—how parents speak to their children, how couples resolve conflict, how individuals choose integrity when compromise would be easier. These moments rarely feel dramatic, but they determine what will be possible later.

A Faith Vanguard builds on truth because truth does not shift when circumstances do. Cultural opinions change. Social trends fade. But what is true remains. When a movement anchors itself in what is eternal, it gains stability. It becomes something people can rely on when everything else feels uncertain. That reliability becomes a refuge.

This foundation is reinforced through teaching and example. People must not only hear what is right—they must see it lived. A Faith Vanguard creates environments where truth is modeled in everyday life. Where faith is visible in how people treat one another, make decisions, and handle hardship. This kind of lived faith becomes a powerful teacher.

Relationships are also part of the foundation. No future is built alone. Strong families create stability. Faithful friendships provide support. Committed communities create resilience. A Faith Vanguard invests in these connections because they are what allow people to endure difficult seasons without losing hope. When people know they are not alone, they are able to keep building even when the work is hard.

Education is another critical element. A Faith Vanguard does not want people who merely repeat what they have been told. It wants people who understand why they believe. It teaches discernment. It encourages thoughtful faith. It prepares people to face challenges with wisdom rather than fear. This kind of formation creates leaders who are ready to carry responsibility.

Laying foundations requires patience. There will be seasons when progress is slow and results are not immediately visible. But what is built carefully is built to last. A Faith Vanguard does not rush what must be rooted. It trusts that steady, faithful work will produce something strong.

The future we are building is not just about success.

It is about sustainability.

It is about creating a faith that can be passed on, a truth that can be trusted, and a community that can stand. When these foundations are secure, whatever rises upon them will be able to endure.

Passing on What Matters Most

The future is never shaped by accident. It is shaped by what one generation chooses to pass to the next. Every belief, every value, and every habit that is not intentionally handed forward is eventually lost. A Faith Vanguard exists because truth is too important to be left to chance. If it is not taught, it will be forgotten. If it is not modeled, it will be misunderstood.

Passing on faith is not primarily about information. It is about formation. People learn what matters by watching what others live. Children learn from their parents. New believers learn from those who walk beside them. Communities learn from their leaders. A Faith Vanguard understands that every life is teaching something, whether it is intentional or not.

This is why example matters more than explanation. A generation raised on speeches but not on integrity will grow cynical. But a generation raised on faith that is lived with consistency will grow strong. They will know what conviction looks like. They will know how to forgive. They will know how to stand. These lessons do not come from books alone. They come from lives that are open and honest.

A Faith Vanguard therefore invests deeply in mentoring. Relationships are formed where wisdom can flow. Older believers share what they have learned. Younger believers bring energy and questions. Together, they grow. This exchange creates continuity. It ensures that truth does not become frozen in one generation, but continues to live and adapt without losing its core.

This process also requires humility. Those who have walked longer must be willing to listen. Those who are just beginning must be willing to learn. When both happen, a powerful culture is formed. It becomes safe to grow. It becomes normal to change. And it becomes possible for faith to deepen over time.

Passing on what matters also means preserving stories. Every community has moments of courage, sacrifice, and faith that deserve to be remembered. These stories remind future generations of what is possible. They show that ordinary people can do extraordinary things when they live with conviction. A Faith Vanguard values these stories because they are part of its identity.

There will be times when the future seems uncertain. Cultural shifts, social pressure, and unexpected challenges will test what has been built. In those moments, what has been passed on will either hold or fail. If faith has been treated as optional, it will fade. But if it has been lived with seriousness and joy, it will endure.

A Faith Vanguard does not try to control the future.

It prepares people to face it.

By passing on truth, values, and courage, it creates a lineage of believers who are ready to stand, build, and lead. That lineage becomes a living bridge between what has been and what will be.

The greatest gift one generation can give another is not comfort.

It is conviction.

Building Something That Will Outlive Us

A future worth inheriting must be built with the long view in mind. Too much of modern life is consumed by what is immediate—quick results, instant feedback, and short-term success. A Faith Vanguard operates on a different timeline. It measures its work not by what it gains this year, but by what it leaves for the next generation.

Everything that lasts is built slowly. Strong families are not formed in a season. Healthy communities are not created overnight. Deep faith is not produced by a single experience. It is cultivated through years of consistent, faithful living. A Faith Vanguard embraces this reality. It chooses endurance over speed and depth over display.

This kind of building requires a willingness to invest without seeing immediate results. Parents plant seeds in children long before they see them grow. Leaders pour into others who may not be ready to lead for years. Communities serve in ways that may never make headlines. But all of these efforts are quietly shaping a future that will one day become visible.

A Faith Vanguard understands that legacy is not about recognition. It is about transmission. What values will still be alive when today's leaders are gone? What truths will still be spoken? What kind of people will the next generation become? These are the questions that guide every decision. They keep the movement focused on what truly matters.

Building something that will outlive us also means creating structures that protect what is being built. Schools, ministries, families, and networks are not ends in themselves. They are vessels that carry truth forward. When they are designed with wisdom and humility, they become powerful tools for preserving faith and community across time.

This work is not glamorous. It often goes unnoticed. But it is sacred. To shape a future where faith is strong, where truth is honored, and where people know who they are is one of the highest callings a person can have. A Faith Vanguard takes this calling seriously.

As each generation builds on what came before, something remarkable happens. The work becomes bigger than any individual. It becomes a shared story of faithfulness. A living testimony to what can be accomplished when people choose to stand, to serve, and to build together.

The future will one day belong to those who are now watching.

What they inherit will be shaped by what we choose to build today.

And when we build with faith, love, and conviction, we create a future that is worthy of them.

Choosing to Be Good Ancestors

One of the greatest questions a person can ever ask is not "What will I accomplish?" but "What will remain because I lived?" Every generation stands on the shoulders of those who came before it. The values we inherit, the freedoms we enjoy, and the faith we carry are all the result of someone else's sacrifice. A Faith Vanguard exists to ensure that we become good ancestors to those who will follow us.

To be a good ancestor means thinking beyond your own lifetime. It means recognizing that your choices today will ripple forward into the lives of people you will never meet. The way you raise your children, the way you treat others, the way you stand for truth—all of these shape the world that future generations will inhabit. A Faith Vanguard invites people to live with that awareness.

Modern culture often teaches people to live for the moment. To seek pleasure, comfort, and recognition now. But this mindset produces fragile societies. When people stop thinking about the future, they stop building anything that lasts. A Faith Vanguard calls us to a deeper vision. It calls us to plant trees whose shade we may never sit under.

Being a good ancestor requires courage. It means making decisions that may not benefit you personally but will bless those who come after you. It means investing time, energy, and resources into things that may not yield immediate rewards. This kind of living goes against the grain of a world obsessed with instant gratification, but it is the kind of living that changes history.

It also requires humility. No one generation has all the answers. We build on what others have done, and we leave work for those who will come next. A Faith Vanguard does not try to finish everything. It tries to begin what matters. It lays foundations that others can strengthen. It passes on wisdom, not control.

Good ancestors also understand the importance of preserving truth. When truth is neglected, it does not disappear—it is replaced. Lies fill the empty spaces. A Faith Vanguard therefore commits to teaching what is true, living what is true, and protecting what is true so that future generations do not have to rediscover it from scratch.

This is not about nostalgia. It is about stewardship. We have been given something precious—faith, freedom, and community. To be good ancestors is to take care of what we have been given and pass it on in better condition than we found it. That is one of the highest forms of love.

The future will not remember our comfort.

It will remember our courage.

A Faith Vanguard chooses to be remembered not for what it consumed, but for what it created. It builds families that are strong, communities that are healthy, and a faith that is alive. These are the gifts that endure.

To live this way is to participate in something far larger than ourselves. It is to join a story that stretches backward and forward through time. And when we choose to be good ancestors, we give the next generation something priceless: a foundation on which they can stand.

That is the future we are called to build.

Standing Faithful Until the Work Is Finished

Building the future is not something that happens in moments of inspiration. It happens through long obedience in the same direction. A Faith Vanguard understands that endurance, not excitement, is what carries a vision forward. There will be seasons when enthusiasm fades, when progress feels slow, and when doubt tries to convince people that their efforts do not matter. But history is not shaped by those who quit when the road becomes difficult. It is shaped by those who remain faithful when the work becomes heavy.

Every generation faces a defining question: Will we keep building, or will we settle for what is comfortable? Drift requires no courage. It happens quietly, through distraction and compromise. But faithfulness requires intention. It requires choosing again and again to stand for what is true even when it would be easier to let go. A Faith Vanguard exists to form people who have that kind of resolve.

There will be moments when standing faithful feels lonely. Not everyone will understand why certain choices are made. Not everyone will see the value of investing in things that do not offer immediate rewards. Leaders may feel misunderstood. Families may feel pressure to conform. Individuals may feel the weight of swimming against the current. A Faith Vanguard prepares people for this reality. It reminds them that they are not called to be popular. They are called to be faithful.

Faithfulness is often quiet. It looks like continuing to pray when answers are delayed. It looks like choosing honesty when deception would be easier. It looks like serving when recognition is absent.

These acts may not make headlines, but they build the kind of character that can sustain a future. Over time, small faithful choices accumulate into something strong.

Community plays a vital role in this endurance. No one is meant to carry the work alone. When one person grows tired, another can step in. When someone stumbles, others can help them stand again. A Faith Vanguard is a people who walk together. They share burdens. They celebrate victories. They remind one another why the work matters when discouragement threatens to take hold.

Standing faithful also means learning how to rest without giving up. Burnout does not build the future. Sustainable faith does. A Faith Vanguard teaches people to care for their souls so they can continue to care for the mission. Rest is not retreat. It is renewal. It allows people to return to the work with clarity and strength.

There will be seasons when the work seems invisible. When seeds have been planted but nothing has yet broken through the soil. These are the moments that test belief. But a Faith Vanguard trusts that growth is happening even when it cannot be seen. Roots are forming. Foundations are being strengthened. The future is quietly being prepared.

The work is never truly finished. Each generation carries it forward in its own way. Some will build new things. Others will protect what has already been built. Others will repair what has been damaged. All of it matters. All of it is part of a larger story that stretches beyond any single lifetime.

In the end, what will matter most is not how quickly we moved, but how faithfully we stood. A Faith Vanguard measures success not by ease, but by endurance. Not by applause, but by obedience. Not by what was gained, but by what was preserved.

When the future looks back, may it see a people who refused to give up.

A people who chose to build when it would have been easier to walk away.

A people who trusted that their faithfulness would shape a world they might never fully see.

That is how the future is built.

When the Future Becomes the Present

There comes a moment in every long work of faith when what once existed only in vision begins to take form in reality. What was spoken in hope is now seen in the world. What was prayed for quietly is now unfolding in front of us. A Faith Vanguard understands that these moments are not accidents. They are the fruit of years of faithfulness, discipline, and perseverance.

When the future begins to arrive, it carries with it both celebration and responsibility. It is easy to rejoice when prayers are answered and dreams take shape. But it is in these moments that a movement is most vulnerable. Growth can create distraction. Success can create complacency. A Faith Vanguard must be especially attentive when things begin to go well, because it is then that the temptation to drift is strongest.

The arrival of the future is not the end of the journey. It is the beginning of a new chapter. What has been built must now be sustained. What has been started must now be stewarded. This requires humility. It requires remembering the long road that led here. It requires honoring the sacrifices that made this moment possible.

A Faith Vanguard does not forget the unseen work that came before the visible fruit. It remembers the prayers that were prayed when no one was watching. It remembers the decisions that were made when the outcome was uncertain. It remembers the people who showed up again and again, even when progress was slow.

These memories anchor the movement in gratitude rather than pride.

As the future becomes the present, new opportunities open. More people become involved. More voices join the conversation. More resources become available. These changes can bring great potential, but they also require greater discernment. A Faith Vanguard must be careful to remain rooted in its original purpose. Growth should strengthen the mission, not dilute it.

This season also brings new responsibilities. Leaders must become more attentive. Systems must become more thoughtful. Communication must become more intentional. But none of these things should replace the heart of the movement. Faith, truth, and community must remain at the center. A Faith Vanguard knows that structures are meant to serve people, not the other way around.

When the future arrives, it also reveals what has been built into the culture. If integrity was planted, it will now be visible. If humility was nurtured, it will now be evident. If truth was honored, it will now be reflected in the way people speak and act. This is the moment when years of formation become visible to all.

A Faith Vanguard embraces this with gratitude. It does not take credit for what God has done. It simply continues to be faithful. It continues to build. It continues to invest in people. The future that has arrived becomes the foundation for what is still to come.

This is the rhythm of faith.

Vision becomes reality.

Reality becomes responsibility.

Responsibility becomes the seed for a new future.

A Faith Vanguard lives in this rhythm with humility and hope. It celebrates what has been built, even as it prepares to build again. Because the work of faith is never finished, and the future is always waiting to be shaped.

· · ·

The Call That Never Ends

There is no finish line for faith. There is no moment when the work is finally complete and the responsibility is laid down forever. A Faith Vanguard exists because the call to stand, to build, and to lead does not expire. Each generation receives the torch, carries it forward, and then passes it on.

What makes a people strong is not that they arrive, but that they continue. They continue to believe when believing is difficult. They continue to build when building is slow. They continue to love when loving is costly. This quiet persistence is what turns vision into legacy.

A Faith Vanguard does not wait for perfect conditions. It moves in faith. It does not wait for certainty. It moves in obedience. And as it moves, the future is shaped by every step taken in trust.

Each person has a role to play. Some will lead from the front. Some will support from behind. Some will work quietly in places no one sees. But all are essential. A Faith Vanguard is not made of spectators. It is made of participants who know that their faith matters.

The call never ends because truth never stops needing to be lived.

Hope never stops needing to be carried.

Love never stops needing to be shown.

The work continues through us, and then beyond us. And in that continuity, a story of faithfulness is written that no single lifetime could ever contain.

PRAYER

· · ·

Father,

Thank You for inviting us into a story that is bigger than our own lives. Give us the faith to keep building when the road is long, the courage to keep standing when it would be easier to retreat, and the humility to know that what we do today shapes tomorrow. Let our lives become faithful bricks in the future You are creating. In Jesus' name, Amen.

REFLECTION

1. Where am I being called to build rather than simply wait?

1. What has God already entrusted to me that I need to steward more faithfully?

2. How do I want my life to shape the future of others?

CHALLENGE

Choose one action this week that invests in the future rather than the moment. It may be mentoring someone, strengthening a relationship, beginning a new discipline, or committing to a long-term goal. Let this be a tangible step toward the future you are called to build.

16

THE LINE THAT SEPARATES THE WATCHERS FROM THE BUILDERS

Every generation eventually reaches a moment of reckoning. A point where comfort and conviction can no longer coexist. It is not always announced with drama. Sometimes it arrives quietly, in the growing sense that something is wrong, that something is slipping, and that continuing as before is no longer an option. History is shaped by these moments, and it is shaped by how people respond to them.

We are living in such a moment now.

We live in a world filled with commentary but starved of commitment. People analyze, debate, and critique endlessly, yet very few are willing to take responsibility for what must be built. It is easier to point out what is broken than it is to repair it. It is easier to talk about change than to become part of it. But the future does not belong to those who watch from a distance. It belongs to those who step forward and act.

This is the line that divides every generation.

The line between those who observe history and those who shape it.

The line between those who wait for someone else to lead and those who become the leaders they were waiting for.

A Faith Vanguard is formed by people who choose to cross that line.

These are not people who think they are special. They are people who know they are responsible. They understand that faith is not something to be admired from afar. It is something to be lived out loud. It is something that demands courage when courage is costly and obedience when obedience is inconvenient.

A Faith Vanguard does not wait for perfect conditions.

It does not wait for consensus.

It does not wait for permission.

It moves because it knows what is at stake.

Every time truth is compromised, something is lost.

Every time faith is treated as optional, something weakens.

Every time good people stay silent, darkness grows bolder.

These realities create a burden. A weight that presses on the conscience of those who still care. That weight is not meant to crush us. It is meant to move us. It is meant to push us out of passivity and into purpose.

This is why a Faith Vanguard exists.

Not to make people feel better,

but to make people stand.

Not to create more voices,

but to create more builders.

The world does not need more observers who can explain what is happening. It needs people who are willing to enter the arena and do something about it. It needs men and women who will speak truth when it is unpopular, who will live with integrity when it is costly, and who will refuse to drift when it would be easier to go along.

This is where the story becomes personal.

Because every person who reads these words is standing at that same line.

You can remain where you are, aware but uninvolved, stirred but unchanged. Or you can step forward and become part of something that matters. Something that will shape the future. Something that will outlast you.

A Faith Vanguard is not an idea.

It is a decision.

And the only question left is whether you will make it.

Why This Moment Cannot Be Delayed

Every age has its excuses. Every generation finds reasons to postpone what it knows must be done. We tell ourselves the timing is not right, that things will eventually improve, that someone else will step in. But history does not move according to our comfort. It moves according to courage. And when courage is delayed, consequences are not.

We are living in a moment that is quietly but unmistakably decisive. The foundations that once held families, communities, and nations together are under strain. Truth is treated as negotiable. Faith is reduced to a private preference. Moral clarity is dismissed as outdated. These shifts do not happen overnight. They happen when enough people decide that standing is too costly and drifting is easier.

A Faith Vanguard exists because drift is no longer harmless.

When truth is treated as flexible, it eventually becomes meaningless. When faith is treated as optional, it eventually disappears. And when responsibility is constantly deferred, something vital is lost. The world does not fall apart all at once. It erodes, one unchallenged compromise at a time.

This is why this moment matters. The longer we wait, the harder it becomes to reverse the damage. The more normalized confusion becomes, the more difficult clarity is to recover. We are not just fighting external pressures. We are fighting internal apathy. And apathy is one of the most powerful forces in human history. It allows decline to feel normal.

A Faith Vanguard calls people to wake up before what has been lost becomes impossible to restore.

There are seasons when speaking is enough. There are seasons when action is required. We are in the latter. The problems we face are not theoretical. They are visible in broken homes, confused identities, fractured communities, and a culture that no longer knows what it stands for. These are not abstract issues. They are the lived reality of millions.

Waiting will not heal this.

Debating will not fix this.

Complaining will not change this.

Only people who are willing to live differently will.

A Faith Vanguard does not pretend to have every solution. But it refuses to be part of the problem. It chooses to embody what it believes. It chooses to create pockets of truth, stability, and faith in a world that desperately needs them.

This moment cannot be delayed because the cost of delay is always paid by the next generation. When adults choose comfort, children inherit confusion. When leaders choose silence, communities inherit chaos. When believers choose convenience, truth becomes harder to find.

We do not get to choose whether the world changes. We only get to choose how we will respond when it does.

A Faith Vanguard is a response. A declaration that we will not drift. A commitment that we will stand.

The future is being shaped right now, by the choices we make today. There will never be a perfect time. There will only be faithful ones. And those who choose to act in this moment will be the ones who define what comes next.

This is why the time is now.

The Kind of People the Future Requires

The future will not be secured by systems alone. It will be shaped by people. Structures can support, laws can regulate, and institutions can guide, but none of these can replace the power of character. What determines whether a society thrives or fractures is not what it builds, but who it becomes. A Faith Vanguard understands that the future is carried on the shoulders of people who are willing to live differently.

Every generation produces individuals of great talent. But talent alone is not enough. The future needs people with conviction. People who know what they believe and why they believe it. People who are not easily swayed by opinion, pressure, or fear. A world that is constantly shifting requires anchors—lives rooted deeply enough to hold when everything else moves.

The future requires people who can think clearly. In an age flooded with information, wisdom has become rare. A Faith Vanguard forms people who can discern what is true, what is good, and what is lasting. They do not chase every new idea. They weigh, test, and examine. They understand that not everything new is progress and not everything old is obsolete.

It also requires people who can love faithfully. The world is not healed by anger alone. It is healed by people who choose to care when it would be easier to withdraw. A Faith Vanguard produces individuals who show compassion without surrendering truth. They know how to be kind without being weak, and how to be strong without being cruel. This balance is one of the most powerful forces in any culture.

The future requires people who are willing to be accountable. Blame is easy. Responsibility is not. A Faith Vanguard forms men and women who own their choices, who admit their mistakes, and who commit to growing. This honesty creates trust. And trust is what allows families, communities, and movements to endure.

It also requires people who are willing to sacrifice. Nothing meaningful is built without cost. Every generation that has preserved freedom, faith, or truth has done so because someone was willing to give up something for something greater. A Faith Vanguard invites people into that same calling. Not to suffer for its own sake, but to invest in something that will outlast them.

These people are not perfect. They are faithful. They stumble. They learn. They keep going. They understand that progress is not about never failing, but about never quitting. This perseverance is what turns ordinary lives into extraordinary legacies.

A Faith Vanguard does not wait for ideal people. It forms them.

Through teaching, through community, and through lived example, it shapes individuals who are ready to carry the weight of the future. These are the people who will raise families with integrity, lead communities with wisdom, and stand for truth when it is under pressure.

The future will belong to those who are prepared for it.

A Faith Vanguard exists to prepare them.

The Cost of Not Standing

. . .

Every generation pays a price for the choices it makes—and for the choices it refuses to make. The greatest cost is not always paid by those who decide to stand, but by those who choose not to. History shows us that silence has consequences. When truth is ignored, it does not simply fade away. It is replaced by something else. And what replaces it is rarely better.

The cost of not standing is first paid in small ways. It appears as quiet compromise. As the slow erosion of values that once seemed unmovable. As the decision to stay comfortable instead of being courageous. Over time, these small choices accumulate. What was once unthinkable becomes normal. What was once wrong becomes tolerated. And eventually, what was once cherished is forgotten.

A Faith Vanguard exists because this pattern is no longer abstract—it is visible. We see it in families that are unraveling, in communities that are fractured, and in a culture that no longer knows what it stands for. These are not random developments. They are the result of years of disengagement. Of people deciding that it was easier to look away than to take responsibility.

The cost of not standing is also paid by the innocent. When those with influence choose silence, those without protection suffer. Children inherit confusion. Communities inherit instability. The vulnerable inherit neglect. These are the hidden casualties of passivity. A Faith Vanguard refuses to accept this as normal.

Standing always carries a price. It may cost comfort. It may cost reputation. It may cost opportunity. But not standing carries a greater cost. It costs truth. It costs clarity. It costs the future. Those losses are far harder to recover.

A Faith Vanguard calls people to see what is at stake. Not to frighten them, but to awaken them. The goal is not to create panic. It is to create responsibility. When people understand that their choices matter, they begin to live differently.

Every person has influence somewhere. In a home. In a workplace. In a community. Choosing not to use that influence is still a choice. And it is a choice that shapes the world just as surely as any action.

The future will not remember who was comfortable.

It will remember who was faithful.

A Faith Vanguard is built by people who are willing to pay the cost of standing so that others do not have to pay the cost of silence.

What Happens When People Choose to Stand

When people choose to stand, the world around them begins to change in ways that are often quiet at first, but powerful over time. Courage has a way of awakening courage. One person who refuses to drift gives permission for others to do the same. A Faith Vanguard grows not through pressure, but through presence—through lives that make conviction visible.

The first thing that changes is the atmosphere. Where confusion once dominated, clarity begins to return. Where fear once silenced voices, truth begins to be spoken. Integrity stops being rare and starts becoming normal. These shifts may seem subtle, but they are foundational. Culture is shaped not only by what is said, but by what is lived.

Standing also creates connection. People who live with conviction recognize one another. They find common ground in their willingness to take responsibility for what they believe. This shared courage builds trust. Trust builds community. And community becomes the place where people are strengthened for the long work ahead. A Faith Vanguard becomes more than a collection of individuals—it becomes a network of mutual support.

As more people stand, momentum begins to grow. Conversations deepen. Relationships are formed across differences. Families begin to change as faith becomes something that is practiced, not just discussed. The movement becomes visible not through noise, but through consistency. People begin to notice that something is different.

Standing also restores hope. In a world that often feels overwhelmed by problems, seeing someone live with integrity reminds others that change is possible. It tells them that they are not trapped by the status quo. That they, too, can choose to live with purpose and clarity.

A Faith Vanguard is built this way.

Not by perfection,

but by persistence.

Not by force,

but by faithfulness.

When people choose to stand, they do more than change themselves. They begin to shape the future.

The Power of Ordinary Faithfulness

History is often told through the stories of extraordinary moments, but it is built through ordinary faithfulness. Revolutions, awakenings, and movements are rarely the result of a single dramatic act. They are the accumulation of countless small decisions made by people who chose to be faithful when it would have been easier to be passive. A Faith Vanguard understands that the future is shaped not just by bold stands, but by daily obedience.

Ordinary faithfulness looks unremarkable from the outside. It looks like parents praying with their children. It looks like people choosing honesty when deception would go unnoticed. It looks like showing up when no one is applauding. These actions may not trend or make headlines, but they form the backbone of a culture that can endure.

A Faith Vanguard values this kind of faithfulness because it is sustainable. Anyone can be courageous for a moment. It takes something deeper to be courageous for a lifetime. When people commit to small acts of obedience every day, those acts begin to compound. Over time, they create character. Character creates trust. Trust creates influence. And influence creates change.

This is why movements that last are always built on simple practices. Prayer. Service. Study. Community. These habits form people who are rooted rather than reactive. They create lives that can weather disappointment without losing direction and success without losing humility.

Ordinary faithfulness also protects people from burnout. When the work is approached as a series of small, faithful steps rather than a single overwhelming task, it becomes possible to keep going. A Faith Vanguard teaches people to focus on what is in front of them, trusting that God will use their obedience to shape what lies ahead.

There will be days when the work feels insignificant. When it seems like nothing is changing. But seeds planted in faith do not fail. They grow in their own time. A Faith Vanguard lives by this truth. It does not measure its impact by immediate results, but by long-term fruit.

Over years, ordinary faithfulness becomes extraordinary. Families are strengthened. Communities are healed. Lives are transformed. What once seemed small becomes something that touches generations.

The world is not changed by flashes of brilliance alone. It is changed by people who refuse to quit.

A Faith Vanguard is built by those who choose to be faithful today, trusting that their obedience is shaping a future they may never fully see.

When Faith Becomes a Public Force

There is a moment when faith moves beyond the private and becomes visible in the world. It stops being something that exists only in the heart and begins to take shape in families, communities, and culture. This is not about display. It is about impact. When people live with conviction long enough, their lives begin to shape the environment around them. A Faith Vanguard exists to carry faith into the public square with humility and courage.

Faith that remains private can be sincere, but it is fragile. It has no structure to protect it. It has no community to reinforce it. It has no voice to defend it. But when faith becomes shared, practiced, and embodied, it becomes resilient. It begins to influence how people treat one another, how they resolve conflict, and how they make decisions. It becomes a stabilizing force in a world that desperately needs one.

A Faith Vanguard understands that this kind of influence does not come from shouting. It comes from consistency. When people live what they believe, their lives become arguments that cannot be easily dismissed. Integrity speaks. Sacrifice speaks. Compassion speaks. Over time, these things become louder than any slogan.

As faith becomes visible, it attracts both curiosity and resistance. Some will be drawn to what they see. Others will feel threatened by it. This is normal. Any force that challenges the status quo will encounter friction. A Faith Vanguard prepares people for this. It teaches them how to remain steady when questioned and gracious when opposed.

Public faith is not about control. It is about contribution. It seeks to serve rather than dominate. It offers truth without coercion. It invites conversation rather than silencing dissent. A Faith Vanguard does not aim to impose belief. It aims to demonstrate its beauty and its strength.

When faith becomes a public force, it begins to heal what has been broken. Families find stability. Communities rediscover trust. People who have been wounded by hypocrisy begin to see a different expression of belief. This is how restoration begins—not through power, but through presence.

A Faith Vanguard carries faith into the world not to win arguments, but to change lives. It understands that love and truth are not opposites. They are partners. And when they walk together, they become a force that can transform even the most fractured places.

A People Who Refuse to Drift

Every generation is shaped by what it tolerates. Over time, what once shocked becomes normal. What once stirred conscience becomes background noise. Drift is rarely noticed in the moment—it happens slowly, through thousands of quiet concessions. A Faith Vanguard exists because too much has been allowed to slip without resistance.

Drift is not always rebellion. Often it is weariness. People grow tired of standing, tired of caring, tired of being different. They begin to tell themselves that a little compromise will not matter. But small compromises always lead somewhere. They create a slope that becomes harder to climb the longer it is walked.

A Faith Vanguard is made of people who recognize this danger and choose to live awake. They refuse to surrender their convictions to comfort. They know that clarity is worth protecting, even when it costs something. They understand that faith that is not lived eventually becomes faith that is forgotten.

Living awake does not mean living angry. It means living intentional. It means asking, in every season, what truth requires. It means refusing to allow convenience to rewrite conviction. These choices are made quietly, day after day, but together they form a life that is steady and strong.

A people who refuse to drift become anchors in their communities. They are not swayed by every new idea or cultural shift. They listen, they discern, and they stand. Others feel safer around them because their lives are predictable in the best way—marked by integrity, faithfulness, and care.

A Faith Vanguard does not seek to be loud. It seeks to be faithful.

And in a world that is constantly shifting, faithfulness becomes a powerful force.

The Quiet Strength That Holds Everything Together

Not all strength announces itself. Some of the most powerful forces in the world move quietly, steadily, without drawing attention. They do not shout. They do not demand recognition. They simply endure. A Faith Vanguard is built on this kind of strength, because it is the only kind that lasts.

Loud movements rise quickly and fall just as fast. They are fueled by excitement, outrage, or trend. But quiet strength is fueled by conviction. It is the strength of people who know what they believe and refuse to let go of it, even when no one is applauding. This is the kind of strength that survives disappointment, opposition, and time.

Quiet strength looks ordinary. It looks like a parent who keeps showing up for their children. A worker who refuses to compromise their integrity. A believer who keeps praying when answers seem distant. These are not glamorous acts. But they are the acts that build a life. And when many lives are built this way, a culture is formed.

A Faith Vanguard understands that character is destiny. When people live with honesty, faithfulness, and humility, those qualities begin to shape everything they touch. Families become steadier. Relationships become healthier. Communities become safer. Not because problems disappear, but because people face them with courage and care.

This kind of strength also creates trust. Trust is not created by words. It is created by consistency. When people know that someone will do what they say, show up when they promise, and treat others with respect, trust grows. And when trust grows, people are willing to invest their lives. This is how movements become more than ideas—they become homes.

Quiet strength also protects against burnout. When people chase attention, they eventually exhaust themselves. When they chase faithfulness, they find a rhythm that can be sustained. A Faith Vanguard teaches people to pace themselves, to rest when needed, and to keep going when the work feels slow. This creates a community that can endure for generations.

There will be moments when standing feels lonely. When voices of compromise seem louder than voices of truth. In those moments, quiet strength becomes a lifeline. It reminds people that they are not alone, even when they feel isolated. It connects them to a deeper purpose that is not dependent on public approval.

Over time, this strength becomes contagious. Others begin to notice. They see lives marked by peace, clarity, and resilience. They see people who are not easily shaken. And they are drawn to it. This is how a Faith Vanguard grows—not through spectacle, but through substance.

Quiet strength does not seek to dominate. It seeks to endure.

And in enduring, it becomes a foundation that can hold everything else.

The Future That Is Now in Your Hands

Every generation reaches a moment when it must decide whether it will merely inherit the world it was given or shape the world that is coming. That moment is not always announced with noise or drama. Often it arrives quietly, disguised as ordinary choices, small conversations, and daily decisions. But those choices are never small. They are the threads from which the future is woven.

A Faith Vanguard exists because this moment is now.

Everything that has been said in these pages leads here—not to agreement, but to action. Not to admiration, but to responsibility. Faith that is only believed is incomplete. Faith that is lived becomes power. The future does not respond to intentions. It responds to obedience.

You do not have to be extraordinary to shape what comes next. You only have to be faithful. The world is not waiting for perfect people. It is waiting for people who are willing to take their convictions seriously. People who will choose truth when lies are easier. People who will choose service when selfishness is rewarded. People who will choose courage when silence would feel safer.

Every place you stand becomes a place where the future is decided.

Every relationship you influence becomes a place where values are formed.

Every choice you make becomes a stone in the foundation of what will come.

A Faith Vanguard is not something that lives on pages. It lives in homes, in communities, in hearts. It lives wherever someone refuses to drift. Wherever someone decides that what is right is worth the cost. Wherever someone takes responsibility for more than just themselves.

The future is shaped in quiet ways. It is shaped when parents teach their children to pray. When workers refuse to compromise their integrity. When neighbors choose compassion instead of indifference. When believers choose to stand even when it feels lonely. These moments do not trend, but they transform.

You may never see the full impact of what you build. You may never know how far the ripples of your faithfulness will travel. But they will travel. They will touch lives you will never meet. They will shape stories you will never hear. This is the mystery and the beauty of obedience—it is never wasted.

A Faith Vanguard understands that the greatest changes are often invisible at first. Roots grow before branches. Foundations are laid before walls rise. What you do today may seem small, but it is not insignificant. It is part of something far larger than you.

This is not a call to retreat from the world.

It is a call to engage it with truth, humility, and courage.

This is not a call to wait for leaders.

It is a call to become one.

The future is not a distant idea.

It is something being written right now, through your choices, your faith, and your willingness to stand.

And that future, in all its possibility and promise, is now in your hands.

PRAYER

Father,

Thank You for calling us into something greater than ourselves. Give us the courage to stand when it is hard, the wisdom to build what will last, and the faith to believe that our obedience matters. Let our lives become instruments of Your truth, and may the future be shaped by Your light working through us. In Jesus' name, Amen.

REFLECTION

1. What truth am I being called to live more boldly?

2. Where have I been hesitant to stand when I know I should?

3. What part of the future is God asking me to help build?

CHALLENGE

Choose one way this week to move from belief to action. Speak truth, serve someone in need, or take a step of obedience that you have been avoiding. Let this be the moment when your faith becomes something that shapes the world.

EPILOGUE
THE STORY BEYOND THE LAST PAGE

Every meaningful story refuses to end where the paper stops. It carries something forward. It leaves behind a weight, a question, a stirring that does not fade when the final sentence is read. Faith Vanguard was never meant to close a chapter—it was meant to open one.

Books can inform. Some can inspire. But the rare ones transform because they invite the reader into something larger than themselves. This is not a book about ideas. It is a book about identity. About who you are when the noise quiets and the moment of decision arrives.

The truth is that history is not shaped by crowds. It is shaped by individuals who decide to live with conviction when it would be easier to drift. The future is not built by movements alone. It is built by people who refuse to surrender their responsibility for what comes next.

Every reader who has come this far is already part of that story.

You have seen the brokenness.

You have felt the weight of what is at stake.

You have recognized that what is being lost matters.

That awareness is not a burden.

It is an invitation.

An invitation to live awake in a world that is drifting.

An invitation to stand when others remain silent.

An invitation to build something that will last.

Faith Vanguard does not ask you to become someone new.

It asks you to become who you were meant to be.

What We Leave Behind

Every life leaves something behind. Even the quietest among us shape the world in ways they may never fully see. The way we love, the way we speak, the way we choose truth or compromise—these things ripple outward. Long after our voices fade, their impact continues.

Most people think legacy is something only the powerful leave. But legacy is not about fame. It is about influence. It is about the values we pass on and the examples we set. A Faith Vanguard understands that what we do in ordinary moments often matters more than what we do in extraordinary ones.

We are always teaching, even when we do not realize it. Children watch how we treat others. Friends notice how we handle hardship. Communities feel the weight of our choices. These quiet lessons accumulate. Over time, they become the culture others inherit.

This is why faith must be lived, not just believed. When faith is visible, it becomes a gift to others. It shows them what is possible. It gives them permission to live with integrity and courage. A Faith Vanguard exists to make this kind of faith contagious.

What we leave behind will not be measured only by what we built.

It will be measured by who we became.

And who we become is shaped by the choices we make every day.

The Quiet Work That Changes Everything

Most of what truly changes the world happens quietly. It does not arrive with applause or recognition. It happens in kitchens, in classrooms, in workplaces, and in moments of private decision. A Faith Vanguard is built not by spectacle, but by these hidden acts of faithfulness.

The small choices are the ones that matter most. Choosing honesty when a lie would be easier. Choosing forgiveness when bitterness would feel justified. Choosing courage when fear is loud. These are the moments that shape a life. And when many lives are shaped this way, a movement begins to form.

The quiet work is often unseen, but it is never insignificant. Every prayer, every act of service, every step of obedience becomes part of something larger. A Faith Vanguard honors this work because it knows that lasting change is always built from the inside out.

You may never know how far the impact of your faithfulness will reach. But it will reach farther than you think.

The Lives We Touch

No one lives in isolation. Every word we speak and every choice we make touches someone else's life. Sometimes the impact is immediate. Sometimes it takes years to be seen. But it is always there. A Faith Vanguard understands that every life is part of a larger story.

The way you live becomes a message to those around you. It tells them what you value. It shows them what you believe is worth standing for. People may forget what you say, but they will remember how you made them feel and what you modeled for them.

This is why kindness matters. Why integrity matters. Why faithfulness matters. These are not small things. They are the threads that weave together families, friendships, and communities. A Faith Vanguard builds these threads carefully, knowing that strong connections create strong futures.

Every person you encounter is part of your legacy.

What you give them—hope, truth, compassion—will travel further than you ever know.

What We Choose to Carry Forward

Every generation decides what it will carry into the future. Some things are preserved with care. Others are left behind. The choices we make about what to keep and what to discard shape the world that follows us. A Faith Vanguard exists because some things are too important to lose.

Truth is one of them.

Faith is another.

Community is another.

These are not guaranteed to survive on their own. They must be protected, practiced, and passed on. When people stop caring, even the most precious things fade. A Faith Vanguard calls us to become guardians of what matters most.

Carrying something forward is an act of love. It means saying that what we have been given is worth preserving. It means choosing to be responsible for more than just ourselves. This is how legacy is built—not through grand gestures, but through faithful stewardship.

What you choose to carry forward will shape the future you leave behind.

. . .

A Future Worth Inheriting

The future does not belong to chance. It belongs to what we prepare for. A Faith Vanguard is built by people who believe that what comes next can be better than what came before. Not because the world will become easier, but because faith, truth, and love will be carried forward with intention.

A future worth inheriting is one where families are strong, where communities are grounded, and where people know who they are and what they stand for. These things do not happen automatically. They are created by the daily choices of ordinary people who refuse to let what matters slip away.

Every act of faithfulness becomes a brick in that future. Every moment of courage strengthens it. Every choice to love when it is difficult makes it more beautiful. A Faith Vanguard is the collective effort of those who believe that tomorrow is worth building today.

The Legacy You Are Writing

Your life is already telling a story. Every choice, every relationship, every act of faith is a sentence being written into it. The question is not whether you will leave a legacy. It is what kind of legacy it will be.

A Faith Vanguard invites you to live with intention. To recognize that what you do today will echo into tomorrow. You may never see the full impact of your faithfulness, but it will be there. In the people you have loved. In the truth you have defended. In the hope you have given.

Legacy is not about being remembered.

It is about making a difference.

And that difference begins now.

Until the Story Is Complete

Every story that matters is bigger than a single life. It stretches beyond one generation, one moment, one set of circumstances. Faith Vanguard was written because the story of faith, truth, and courage is not finished. It is still being told through the lives of those who choose to stand.

You are part of that story now. Not as a reader, but as a participant. What you do with what you have been given will shape the chapters that follow. The future will remember the people who refused to drift, who chose to love, and who believed that what they did mattered.

This is not an ending.

It is a beginning.

And the story continues with you.

ABOUT THE AUTHOR

Scott Farley is the founder of Faith Vanguard, a movement dedicated to restoring clarity, courage, and conviction in a world that has grown comfortable with confusion. His work is rooted in the belief that faith is not meant to be passive, private, or powerless—it is meant to be lived boldly, practiced daily, and carried forward with purpose.

Scott's writing and leadership emerge from a lifelong commitment to truth, spiritual discipline, and the responsibility each generation holds to shape the future. He does not write from a distance. He writes from the front lines of faith—where belief is tested, where culture presses back, and where courage must be chosen again and again.

Faith Vanguard was born from a simple realization: too many people see what is wrong, but too few feel called to build what is right. Scott's message is not one of despair, but of awakening. He challenges readers to move beyond observation into participation, to stop waiting for change and become part of it.

Through Faith Vanguard, Scott works to equip individuals, families, and communities to stand in truth with humility, strength, and love. His mission is to help people rediscover who they are, what they believe, and why it matters—not just for their own lives, but for the generations that will follow.

Scott lives by a conviction that guides everything he does:

Faith is not something you admire.

It is something you live.

This book is an invitation to do exactly that.

FAITH VANGUARD — THE NEXT STEP

You did not pick up this book by accident.

Something in you recognized that what the world is offering is not enough. Something in you knew that faith, truth, and responsibility still matter. That awareness is not random. It is a calling.

Faith Vanguard is not a slogan.

It is a movement.

It is a growing community of people who have decided to stop drifting and start building. People who refuse to surrender their convictions to comfort. People who understand that faith is not meant to be private or passive—it is meant to be lived boldly and carried forward with purpose.

This book was never meant to be the end of your journey. It was meant to be the beginning of it.

What Comes Next

If these pages stirred something in you, it is because you were meant to be part of what is being built.

Here are your next steps:

1. Stay Connected

Visit FaithVanguard.org to join the community, receive updates, and stay connected to the growing movement.

2. Join the Vanguard

Sign up for the Faith Vanguard newsletter and receive teachings, reflections, and updates designed to keep you grounded, focused, and moving forward.

3. Share the Message

If this book spoke to you, pass it on. Give it to someone who needs clarity, courage, or direction. Movements grow when people share what matters.

4. Live It

The most important step is not online—it is personal.

Stand for truth.

Live with integrity.

Build what will last.

You Are Not Alone

Faith Vanguard is made of ordinary people who chose to be faithful. You do not have to have everything figured out. You only have to be willing to take the next step.

The future is being shaped by those who refuse to drift.

Welcome to the Vanguard.

A LETTER TO THE READER

Dear Friend,

If you have made it this far, I want to begin with something simple and sincere: thank you. You did not have to read this book. You did not have to give it your time, your attention, or your heart. Yet you did. That tells me something about you. It tells me that you care. That you are paying attention. That somewhere inside you is a hunger for something more solid, more true, and more meaningful than what the world is offering.

I wrote Faith Vanguard because I could no longer ignore what I was seeing around me. Families drifting. Communities fractured. Faith reduced to a slogan instead of a way of life. Too many people sensing that something is wrong, but not knowing what to do about it. I was one of them.

This book was born out of that tension — the tension between what is and what could be. I am not a perfect man. I do not have all the answers. But I do know this: truth matters. Faith matters. And the future is too important to leave to drift.

There came a moment in my own life when I realized that waiting for someone else to step forward was no longer an option. If something was going to be built, someone had to begin. Faith Vanguard began as a quiet conviction — a belief that ordinary people, living with integrity and courage, could shape something extraordinary together.

What you have read in these pages is not theory. It is a call. A call to live awake in a world that is numbing itself. A call to stand when silence would be easier. A call to build something that will outlast us.

You may not feel ready. You may not feel qualified. That's okay. None of us ever truly are. But readiness has never been what changes the world. Willingness does.

I believe that you are reading this because you are willing.

You don't have to have everything figured out. You only have to take the next step. To live your faith a little more boldly. To love a little more intentionally. To stand a little more firmly in what you know is true.

Faith Vanguard is not about me. It is about us — people who refuse to drift, who choose to build, and who believe that what we do today shapes what tomorrow becomes.

Thank you for being part of this story.

With hope and resolve,

Scott Farley

A CLOSING BLESSING

May this book not fade when the cover closes.

May the words you have read become something you live.

May the courage stirred in these pages find its way into your choices, your conversations, and your daily steps forward.

May you walk with clarity in a world that often chooses confusion.

May you stand with quiet strength when the pressure to compromise grows.

May you love with depth when it would be easier to withdraw.

May your faith be more than something you hold — may it be something you practice.

May your home become a place of peace and truth.

May your relationships be marked by honesty and grace.

May your work be done with integrity.

May your life become a steady light to those who are searching for direction.

May you remember that you are not called to be perfect — only faithful.

May you have the courage to keep going when the road is long.

May you find rest when you are weary and purpose when you are unsure.

May you never forget that what you do matters, even when it feels small.

May the seeds you plant today grow into something beautiful tomorrow.

May the love you give return in ways you could never have imagined.

May the truth you live become a foundation others can stand on.

May the legacy you leave be one of faith, hope, and courage.

And when you are tempted to drift,

may you remember why you chose to stand.

When you are tempted to be silent,

may you remember the power of your voice.

When you are tempted to give up,

may you remember the future that is still being built.

You are part of something larger than yourself.

You are part of a story that is still unfolding.

You are part of a Vanguard that refuses to fade.

May you walk forward with confidence.

May you build with patience.

May you lead with humility.

May you live with conviction.

And may the God who called you into this story

walk beside you every step of the way.

Amen.

www.ingramcontent.com/pod-product-compliance
Lightning Source LLC
Chambersburg PA
CBHW020539030426
42337CB00013B/911